The Team

Formula

A Leadership Tale of a Team

who Found their Way

By Mandy Flint & Elisabet Vinberg
Hearn

Paperback ISBN 9781780923475
ePub ISBN 9781780923482
PDF ISBN 9781780923499
Published in the UK by MX Publishing
335 Princess Park Manor, Royal Drive, London, N11 3GX

www.mxpublishing.co.uk (UK & Europe)
www.mxpublishing.com (USA)

Cover design by www.staunch.com

Disclaimer:

This is a work of Fiction. Any similarity to persons living or dead (unless explicitly stated) is merely coincidental.

Acknowledgements

There are so many people we want to acknowledge, who, in different ways have inspired us, helped us and supported us in our careers and development, and in writing this book.

Thank you, Julian and Rich and the rest of our families for all your tireless support and unwavering belief in our ability to make this book dream a reality. Don't order the Bentley and Aston Martin quite yet! ☺

Thank you, Sophie Brown, for your prompt and meticulous editing that helped us enhance this book.

Thank you, Maximilian and Daniel, for occasionally joining us in our Skype calls and adding some inspiration, wearing post-it notes on your faces ☺.

Thank you, Glennis, for being our sales guru and constantly reminding us that anything is possible.

Thank you, Sue and Nicki, for helping us create and target our book proposal, which means this book now exists.

Thank you, Mark Shelmerdine, for so generously sharing your knowledge and experience from the publishing world with us.

Thank you, Steve Emecz of MX Publishing, for believing in us and our book.

Thank you, Bill Barton, Barry and Su Robertson, for playing a major part in our personal and professional development journey. Without your guidance and influence, we wouldn't be where we are today.

Thank you to all the people, clients and colleagues, we've had the privilege and pleasure to work with over the years. You have taught us so much.

And finally a big thank you to all our friends who have inspired and encouraged us and helped us in more ways than you will ever know. A special remembrance-thank you to the late John Cordiner who made us think about the relationships in the book.

Mandy and Elisabet

Contents

How to read this book

There are two ways of reading this book.

1. Open the book, read the book, be entertained, close the book.
2. Open the book, read the book, be entertained, reflect on how the book applies to you by using the reflection/discussion questions, apply your learnings. Then close the book.

We recommend the second option! ☺

Chapter 1: The Merger

"It will all be OK in the end. If it's not OK, it's not the end."

Unknown

"I have had enough! I am so frustrated and nervous. What on earth is happening here? These rumours have been going around for ages. I have just had enough."

Stephen had been trying all day, unsuccessfully, to push the thought of the rumours away. Now he got out of his chair and started to pace up and down the length of his small office to try and physically shift the thought out of his head. It didn't work.

"Rumours are a killer. They slow everyone down, people speculate, time gets wasted and, to be perfectly honest, people just get distracted from their jobs" thought Stephen. *"Look, I am even doing it myself, right now."* This really annoyed him. Stephen was the type of person who just wanted to get the job done and he wanted to do it well.

"We've had enough of rumours now. We just need to know" thought Stephen to himself. He was unable to shake the pondering. *"I need to know."*

Tightrope Insurance, who Stephen worked for, had been having financial problems for some time, with progressively dwindling profits. Rumours had it that the Tightrope leaders had been talking to Black Sparrow Insurance about a potential merger. This was a great worry to Tightrope's employees, as Black Sparrow had a bad reputation in the industry for having an old-fashioned dictatorial leadership style. In fact, a number of Tightropers had worked for Black Sparrow. Their stories and experience were widely known; the company was infamous. Black Sparrow Insurance wasn't dubbed *BS* for nothing.

There was Anna. Anna had joined Stephen's team from BS nine months earlier. She hadn't really told Stephen about what had happened as it wasn't Anna's style to confide in just anybody. Over time though, Stephen had pieced most of it together. Her story was very similar to others he had heard. Of course, he realised that some of them may have been embellished through re-telling, as was usually the case when people had grievances, but the picture was still pretty clear.

When Anna was at BS she had had some of the common complaints that people have about their managers:

- Not communicating enough. Anna needed and wanted to know more about what was going on and how it all connected together, but her leader simply wasn't telling her. She was getting frustrated and kept finding out important information from other people when her leader really should have been the one telling her.

- Not getting support. Not getting any feedback. Anna craved support from her leader and a big part of that was getting feedback on what she was doing well and what she could do better. Plus, most importantly, _how_ she could do better.

- No team meetings. The team really wanted meetings but the leader decided not to get people together. Instead, people would be given small pieces of information which meant that the approach was not coordinated. Consequently, people felt left out and were unable to understand why they were carrying out activities and tasks. It was like being in a maze.

- No one-to-ones. Anna had not had meetings with her boss. Having them would have allowed her a natural forum to talk about her work and progress.

- Not understanding how the decisions got made. Most decisions had seemed hap-hazard to her; disjointed and unclear.

- Being asked to do things that didn't make sense, where she just couldn't see the connection. As a result, she found it hard to get engaged and involved.

Anna, with her natural dedication and loyalty, kept going for four years like that; getting by but not progressing much, noticing that she was passed up for promotions but not quite realising why. You could argue that she wasn't very good at picking up the political undertones, that she didn't understand the 'unwritten rules', such as always agreeing with the boss. Or maybe she had understood, but she just wasn't a person to play games; she was too honest for that. So the eventual outcome was pretty given. She walked out the door and kept walking ... until she ended up at Tightrope.

The breaking point had come one day when her manager started shouting at her in front of the team. Anna had been horrified and deeply hurt and angry. Not only did she feel that she had not had any feedback on anything she had done but now, all of a sudden, her manager was shouting at her, accusing her of dropping the ball on a customer issue, which was totally untrue.

"But that is really unfair and untrue." Anna had stammered, not quite believing what she was hearing.

"What are you basing that on?" she continued.

The room went deadly silent and Anna's boss looked at her coldly.

"I told you personally to take care of this customer"

Silently Anna had caught her breath, in shock. She knew this was a blatant lie and so did everyone else. In fact, it was the boss herself who had dropped the ball and was now blaming Anna in order to save her own skin. She hadn't expected that kind of behaviour, even from her boss, even though she didn't trust her. From that moment it had been obvious that there was nowhere to go with this. It would be pointless to challenge her manager, who would never admit to the lie. Anna couldn't see any point in escalating it either. She didn't trust that the organisation would support her. "*Who was she to think anyone would back her at the cost of her manager who was more senior and seen as an 'up and coming' leader,"* she had thought. No, she had known that was it.

Anna had felt crushed; the other team members had withdrawn and hadn't supported her (even though they knew the boss was wrong). So it had been time for Anna to move on. It had become both painful and pointless to stay. The years of neglect and unfair leadership came to a head at that point, like a pressure-cooker exploding. It was the final straw. She didn't want to be a part of it anymore.

She decided that it should feel good to come to work but there it just didn't, and it hadn't done for so long. She handed in her notice that evening. She quit.

"What if the rumours are true, what would it be like to merge with BS?" thought Stephen. He was happy to receive the announcement about the Town Hall meeting with 'mandatory attendance' but was a little anxious nonetheless.

"Mandatory attendance! That must mean that there is something very special going on", he thought.

From his window seat he spotted the bustling London street below him; people were busily getting on with their lives while Stephen was left worrying.

He wondered what would happen at this meeting, if he would still be looking out of this window at the end of tomorrow. He'd been at this desk since being promoted to a

Director only last year, taking on the responsibility for the Central Europe and Scandinavia service teams. He liked his job. He liked working for the company, he liked the challenges and everything he had learned over his five years of service. Maybe it hadn't been the kind of progress that he would have hoped for, partly because of the many changes that just seemed to have made people risk-averse and hesitant to really take action. Nevertheless, it was still a good job, he was paid well and he enjoyed it.

"So it's another change", Stephen thought, *"the other changes haven't really had that much of an impact on me or my team. I have got a different feeling about this one though. If we merge, what does that mean for me? There will be too many people."*

He got up to go home. Tomorrow he hoped he would finally find out if the rumours had been true.

Stephen's Journal

So, this journal is finally going to see the light of day. Alice will be delighted; she gave it to me and has waited for me to start it for a long time. She seems to think it will do me good to write things down. Not so sure about that. Anyway, let's see how this goes.

I am torn. I can't stop thinking about the fact that I might lose my job and I know that everyone else is probably thinking the same thing. At the same time we need to carry on as usual. This is really hard.

I'm going to have to talk to them about not letting this affect our productivity somehow. I've got my boss breathing down my neck about the latest stats; we need to improve these results. And I've said I can do it, so I've got to do it.

I am relieved that I am going to this mandatory meeting tomorrow. I am pretty sure there will be answers and whatever they are, I will deal with it. I just want to move on and get some clarity, to know where I am going. I want to find my way.

I seriously need to think about something else now. This is too energy draining. I need some distraction! I think I'll go and find Alice. Maybe see if she wants to watch a fun movie and then I can tell her I have started this journal. Watch this space.

Chapter 2: Coming together

"A team in name alone is not a team."

"Welcome to our first team meeting".

The words were Stephen's as he looked around the table, trying to take in what he had in front of him. This was the first time the new team was gathered in the same room; some of his old team members and the new people from BS.

When the merger was announced, in that Town Hall meeting a few months ago, Stephen would never have imagined himself sitting with these five people around the table as their leader. His first thought had been "*they will need to merge my team with our BS counterpart and their leader has longer tenure. He'll be the one to get the new leadership job*". He considered himself very lucky when the BSer had decided to leave as a result of this merger, and he, Stephen, was appointed the leader of the new team.

Naturally there had been redundancies. This had been one of the reasons for the merger; to run a tighter ship with lower overheads. Two of Stephen's old team had had to go and the same had happened at BS. This was of course not what Stephen would have wanted, but he had no say in the matter and he felt reasonably comfortable that the people in question would find new positions elsewhere within the next year. Nevertheless, he shook off the slight feeling of unease that this chain of thought had created.

As he looked around the table he sensed resistance and, at the same time, some excitement. He noticed how Anna was being particularly quiet, not really looking at any of the others. His gaze moved to JR who was tapping his pen impatiently against the big table. Samuel on the other hand looked bored, as if he had something better to do than being in this meeting.

Stephen had been hoping that this was going to be a relatively straightforward process, although somehow he sensed that it was not going to be quite that simple. He had spent a fair amount of time preparing the agenda, but no time thinking about how to approach the team members or how they would be when they came together like this.

They were all seated in comfortable black office chairs around an oval boardroom style table. It was one of those rooms with no windows, placed in the centre of the building, on the 7th floor of the BS office. This was where the London people were now all based. The Tightrope building had been vacated. The walls were decorated with an eclectic collection of modern art mixed with posters of the old BS corporate values.

"I imagine those values will need to be updated", thought Stephen, before directing his attention back to the team, annoyed at his own inability to keep focused in this important first meeting.

In the spirit of cost cutting, coffee and tea were all that were on offer: the biscuits had gone.

"Are we getting any biscuits? At Tightrope we used to get really good chocolate muffins and biscuits". Samuel said, in a superior way.

"Maybe that's why you're now in our building? You couldn't manage your costs" said JR with his strong New York accent and a wry smile.

Stephen choked on his coffee. "*This isn't going to be easy*" he thought.

"Come on guys, let's get this meeting started", Stephen said abruptly, desperately trying to ignore the comments and the hostility that hung in the air.

"Let's go around the room and introduce ourselves. I know some of you have met before, but this is our first team meeting together, so let's do it right." As JR sat on his right, he waved his hand towards him and said: "Can you start, JR?"

"Sure. Hi guys. Great to be here. I'm JR. As you know, I'm an original Black Sparrow employee; been with BS for 15 years. I'm the Head of Customer Services for Americas, out of New York. I have an awesome team; we've delivered on every target since I took over the team 4 years ago. Got a good team behind me. I'm real excited that we've taken over Tightrope, and I'm sure that we're gonna make this a success".

As JR looked at his new colleagues, he wondered how much he actually needed this group, if at all, once back in New York. New York was different anyway and far away from the rest of this group.

The tension in the room mounted, as JR branded the merger as a takeover.

*"Arrogant b*****d"*, Samuel thought, *"but then what else is new"*.

"As you all know, I am Samuel – the longest serving employee here. I've been with Tightrope for 23 years, and I'm heading up the UK Customer Services team, who are a highly respected, experienced group of individuals. I've seen it all, changes, new leaders, the latest management trends: there's nothing I haven't seen. You'll get to know me. Everyone at Tightrope calls me for my expertise. This *merger"*, he emphasised, "will, I expect, be like the other two that I've seen: it won't make much difference to my situation, but I am prepared to share my expertise for the good of this new company".

Secretly Samuel had no intention of sharing his knowledge. *Why should he?* He had worked hard for it, and he didn't want some new kids on the block to shine at his expense, so he would be very careful with what he shared. For now he would play the game. He was good at that; he'd done it for 23 years.

The room fell silent, and everyone looked to Christine. It was her turn, but Christine didn't notice. Instead, she was studying her Blackberry under the table. She looked tired and drawn.

"Christine?" Stephen prompted.

Christine looked up, slowly, put her Blackberry down, and sighed quietly.

"My name is Christine. I used to work in the Paris office before they closed it down 2 years ago as part of the BS centralisation. I'm now based here in London, responsible for MIS and IT projects, and I've obviously worked with all of you already. We have major changes ahead of us on the systems side, and this is going to impact all of you and your customers, so watch this space – you'll hear a lot from me."

Christine felt distracted. There was just too much going on; she should be at home. Her work had caused enough problems at home as it was. But she didn't want to think about that now. That last message on her Blackberry had rattled her. She had to force herself to pay attention.

Inwardly Stephen groaned, turning to Anna with a hopeful smile.

"I'm Anna, Head of Customer Services for Scandinavia, based in Stockholm. I have a lovely hard-working team. I wholeheartedly support this merger and I'm looking forward to working with all of you. I'm so pleased that Stephen got the position of heading up this global team. He's a great leader and –"

Christine interrupted Anna mid-sentence, "Didn't you used to work at BS?"

"Um. Yes, I did, a few years ago now. I guess that I'm the only one here that has worked at both companies". Anna didn't really want to talk about her time at BS, so she hoped that would be enough. Christine didn't say anything more. Anna was relieved. She reflected on her new colleagues, looking around the table. It felt good to be part of this new group. Sure, some of them seemed a bit more confrontational than she felt comfortable with, but she was sure this was just down to the newness of the team. It would get better.

"And last but not least", Stephen said – "here's Sophia"

Sophia's bubbly personality showed from the start. With a big smile on her face, she had been eager to talk from the beginning:

"Yes, I'm Sophia, Head of Customer Services for the rest of Europe and I'm also based here in London. I get to work with a number of great countries, like Hungary, Greece and Russia, to mention just a few, although most of the servicing happens out of London. I love my job" and they could all see that she meant it, her eyes were dancing and she was somehow exuding boundless energy. She continued, "I personally think that this is a great opportunity for all of us. I really want this to work. I have learned a lot from my 7 years at BS and I'm confident that we can take the best of both worlds and create something special. I'm proud to take on this new leadership role, it'll be very interesting".

What Sophia didn't share was that she was frankly a whole lot more excited than she could let on (as some of the others seemed a bit negative). She didn't like the BS culture and she hoped that the merger could change that culture.

The meeting that followed was polite. The agenda seemed to be flowing smoothly, with people listening and Stephen doing most of the talking. Then the subject of the financial situation came up. Stephen had dreaded this, fearing that some of the team members might get defensive.

"Let's review the financials. We are losing money and we have to turn this around. We need to take a long, hard look at how we do things around here. We must cut costs. I suggest we look at the details of the figures and try to work out where things have gone wrong."

The reaction in the room was one of defence as they all started thinking about how they were going to justify their figures. The politeness turned into finger-pointing and before Stephen knew it, the meeting had turned sour. He didn't quite know how this had happened or how to turn it around again. Not knowing what else to do, he simply focused on getting some actions and next steps agreed, and then, closing the meeting.

He couldn't wait to get out of there. Managing this team was a puzzle he was going to have to solve as soon as possible.

Stephen's Journal

Wow, well that didn't go very well, in fact not at all the way I expected it to go! What on earth am I doing? I thought I had it all in hand. It just didn't go the way I wanted it to.

Alice said I should write down in this journal how I feel when things don't go as I expect. I am going to give it a go.

I don't know why everyone got so defensive. I got a sinking feeling in the pit of my stomach when that happened. They all just seemed to focus on their own area; they just weren't interested in finding solutions or thinking about each other. Why can't they just work together, the way I want them to? I have to think of something new. They're all so stuck in their own ways; the old BSers think that BS is best and the old Tightrope team think that they're the best. How am I going to make this work? I can see the best of both worlds, why can't they see it too? I have to think about how I can make them see what I see. Maybe I should be more prepared for these defensive reactions when I am in meetings? Perhaps I could spend more time preparing for how they will react before the next meeting?

Helmut is demanding more from me and keeps telling me we have to improve our results. If I don't get this sorted out it seems like Helmut will have my head on a plate.

I have to admit, I'm feeling a little unsure about this job. I keep asking myself, can I really do this? I mean they had no choice but to give me the job. Does Helmut want me to succeed? I am just not sure about this right now. That meeting has unsettled me, no, come on I can do this. I know what to do. This is just a small set back. I can lead them through this.

Alice thinks I should give myself time and not be so tough on myself, but she wasn't there, she didn't experience what I did.

I want this to work so badly! What can I do? I wonder if there is anyone I could talk to? Can't really talk to my boss – Helmut's not interested in the details, he expects me to just sort it out, so that we turn the results around.

Is this working, writing this down? Feels like I'm just highlighting my failures. No, actually, I think writing this down has made me feel a bit better.

There must be a solution. I've done some team building before, maybe that's what we should do? Yeah, let me think about that some more.

Chapter 3: The emails – the set-up

"The world is all gates, all opportunities, strings of tension waiting to be struck."

Ralph Waldo Emerson

Dear all,

After the meeting and the review of the figures, I've decided we need to spend more time working on us as a team. On reflection I have realised that we need to improve our understanding of what everyone's roles and responsibilities are and get to know each other better. This will help us to be more successful as a team and, therefore, achieve our results.

For that reason, I have decided that we will do some team building at our next team meeting, which will take place in Stockholm 5th of June.

I will liaise with Anna to work out the details of the venue and the contents. Please let Anna know if you have any ideas for this team building that you would like us to take into consideration.

In the meantime, please continue your focus on cutting costs. See if you can come up with any ideas for how the processes in your team can be improved and become more effective, as this will also help reduce costs. Feel free to discuss with each other and share thoughts if appropriate.

Helmut and I will be reviewing the figures again next week, so please send me your data and any suggestions by Friday. This should leave me enough time to go through them before my meeting with Helmut next Tuesday. Thank you.

Regards,

Stephen

Hi Steve

Great idea. I'll be there.

See you in Stockholm

Regards,

JR

Hi Stephen

I'm not sure I can make this date. I have some important meetings so feel free to go ahead without me. You can brief me afterwards.

Regards,

Christine

Hi Stephen!

I think this is a great thing to do. It will really help the team.

My suggestion for contents is that we should share best practices. I've seen some great things that work at BS and some other great things at old Tightrope. If we all shared these practices, we could all benefit from them. So maybe we should make this into a 2 day event so that we have enough time? What do you think?

Thanks,

Sophia

Dear all,

I'm pleased you are all coming to Stockholm – it's beautiful this time of year!

I've looked into options for the venue and I've found what I think could be a great choice. It's an old manor house outside the city with access to quad bikes and a sauna. For those who are brave, you can also swim in the (cold) sea. ☺

Thanks for your thoughts so far. If you haven't yet given your input, there is still time to do so.

Regards,
Anna

Dear Christine

I want you to reschedule the meetings that are currently stopping you from attending the team building. I need everyone there and I expect you to be there too.

Thanks,

Stephen

Dear Sophia

Thanks for your input. At this point we can't really justify taking 2 days out, so I think an agenda which includes roles and responsibilities and the element of fun will be enough.

Regards,
Stephen

Dear all

The team building will go ahead in Stockholm as planned on the 5th of June. We plan to arrive the evening before, so please book your flights accordingly. Anna will send you the details of the venue separately.

We will spend the morning sharing roles and responsibilities and getting to know each other. In the afternoon we will all ride quad bikes around the countryside. If you haven't done it before, it's really easy and a lot of fun! We will finish with dinner and sauna.

I look forward to seeing you all there.

Regards,
Stephen

Stephen's Journal

I feel like I have had a good day today. With all those emails flying around about the team building I think I have got them excited, or at least I have told them we are going to do it.

Why haven't I heard from Samuel on this team build? He doesn't seem to get involved much at all. He's a bit full of himself – but then he always was, wasn't he? I wonder how this will impact the team. My instinct tells me I need to keep an eye on him. I am not sure that I can trust him.   Anna seems keen to make this team session a success and she is trying to get the others to join in with the planning, I like that.

But why haven't they all talked to each other about the figures? I asked them to but they seem to just do their own thing and then they each come and talk to me about their own part of it. I need to get them talking, although maybe too much talking will just stir things up? I don't want another meeting like the last one. It might just be easier to keep them away from each other.

But then we have the team building coming up... What can I do to make it smooth and non-confrontational? That's what I need to figure out.

Alice said that the quad bikes are a good idea, we can have a bit of fun together too. I like the idea of that.

Chapter 4: Quad bikes in the archipelago

"The way a team plays as a whole determines its success. You may have the greatest bunch of individual stars in the world, but if they don't play together, the club won't be worth a dime."

Babe Ruth

"So, where is Samuel?" Anna looked at the others. "We said we would meet at 2 and it's already 10 past. Where is he?"

Stephen tried not to look frustrated, but was finding it hard. The morning team building had been OK, but not much more. Frankly it had been a bit dry and not as dynamic as he had hoped; he was quite relieved that it was finally over. Now he wanted to shake that off and was ready to have some fun. Even if the team hadn't bonded much so far, he was sure this would do it. *"There's nothing quite like some friendly competition to get people to get to know each other better"*, he thought.

They were all, apart from Samuel, standing by the quad bikes. To their right was the manor house, a big white rendered building with big windows and a large terrace with uninterrupted views of the sea. The adjoining crop fields were lit by the sun; it was a beautiful Swedish summer day. To their left the quad bike trail disappeared around the corner on top of the sea cliffs, into the next bay.

The morning session had started smoothly and uneventfully. They had gone around the table sharing what they do, asking each other some questions for clarification when needed. This seemed to help the group gain insight into each other's areas. It had, however, also highlighted that there were both gaps and overlaps between the team members. JR had been pleasantly surprised by how much he had learnt and he had come to the conclusion that there could well be some benefits to being part of the group. Sophia had been keen to share. She had done so openly and had expected the same back; yet she wasn't convinced that the others had been as open.

Stephen's phone bleeped. He picked it up and hit the keypad to reveal a text message:

"Obviously I'm not coming to the quad bikes as I have a bad back. I'm going to be working in my room at the manor and I'll see you at dinner. Samuel"

Stephen was shocked, *"what was this? How come Samuel had not said anything about this before, and they had been together all morning?"* He became aware of the team looking at him. He looked up, making an effort not to show how annoyed he was. He had to demonstrate leadership right now.

"Samuel's not coming. He has a bad back. He'll see us later at dinner. So let's get going and have some fun".

This was an awkward moment for the team and everyone remained still for a few seconds. It was as if time stood still momentarily. The element of shock that Stephen had experienced sent a ricochet around the circle where they had gathered, standing facing each other. JR raised his eyebrows in surprise but said nothing as he glanced over at Sophia for a response. Sophia looked down, not knowing if she should respond but wanting to display her surprise too.

They moved silently towards the bikes and began mounting their own allocated quad bikes. They ignited the engines, then, slowly and cautiously started following the quad bike guide who set off along the track. As the scenery passed them by, all of them soon forgot about Samuel, and everything else for that matter, caught up in the excitement of the speed and the sense of freedom. As she glanced at the glittering sea, Sophia shouted: "Magnifico! Bellissimo!" She was a racing driver at heart; that much was clear. JR and Stephen saw that Sophia was picking up speed and their competitive spirits kicked in. They raced to catch up with her, screaming: "This may be how you drive in Italy, but we can still beat you!"

The afternoon proceeded with a lot of merriment; the group was chasing each other around, having lots of fun and not paying much attention to what the guide was pointing out to them.

Stephen didn't seem to notice that Christine kept trailing behind, occasionally getting her Blackberry out, an air of uncertainty about her. She would regularly stop and gaze at her phone. She checked her messages with a sigh, looking uncomfortable at whatever news she was getting. Then, slowly, she would drop her Blackberry back into her pocket, thoughtfully zipping it safely away. After gazing into the horizon with a defocused look in her eyes she would reluctantly carry on after the others, staying at the back of the group as they weaved their way across the countryside.

Late in the afternoon they stopped at a deserted headland, where they had some drinks and a well-deserved break. The headland jutted out into the rolling sea; the waves had turned it into the point of a knife, cutting into the white surf below. The team ending up sitting on the grass, overlooking the rocks as the waves crashed down, pushing water up onto the jagged stones. It was moment of reflection.

Stephen turned to JR. "What did you think of this morning?"

"I enjoyed it", he said, "I think this could be a good team if we're all in it for the same reason". The question mark hung in the air. "What did you think?"

"Yeah, good", replied Stephen. "I feel positive about it, but I think we need to do some work to align the responsibilities, that became clear to me today".

Stephen had a niggling thought at the back of his mind that there was something he had overlooked in the morning session. He couldn't put his finger on it, but something was not quite right.

Sophia, with a big smile, added, "This morning was great. I really enjoyed it. I got to know so much about what my colleagues do. It's been really helpful. It feels like we're a team". Christine nodded her agreement, but said nothing. Anna was happy; it all seemed to go well. She'd even managed to make the sun come out, she thought, smiling to herself.

They drove back with the sun still high in the sky, even though it was past six o'clock already. They'd had a great afternoon. There was a buzz around them as they dismounted the bikes and walked towards the terrace for drinks. They were jostling with each other and there was a cheerful banter between them that made them move freely and easily onto the terrace.

Anna was the first person to spot Samuel. He was sitting on the terrace with his head down, staring into his Blackberry.

"Hey Samuel" she called out "we missed you today. And you missed out on a great afternoon. How's your back?"

Samuel managed to pull his head up from his Blackberry and said, with a smirk, "I've been working. I just have a lot on right now and quad bikes are not for me or my back".

As he said this, JR walked back from the bar with a drink, slapping Samuel on the back, saying "Hey buddy, you missed some fun. The sea was real beautiful and I beat Sophia in the racing!" He smiled over at Sophia who returned the smile saying, "I'll get you next time, don't you worry". The others chuckled. It had become very obvious that both Sophia and JR were immensely competitive.

If Samuel had thought about it, he probably would have felt left out, but he didn't really care. Stephen was still angry with Samuel. He knew he would need to talk to him about what had happened that afternoon, yet he also knew that now was not the time. It would have to wait.

The friendly banter continued all through dinner. Overall, spirits were high and people seemed relaxed; the team had finally started to bond. They sat on the terrace, overlooking the sea as the sun was finally setting. There was a chill in the air but they didn't really notice or mind. The conversation had drifted from favourite holidays back onto the subject of work and the customer they had recently lost.

"I've had a great idea about how we could save money. We produce too many Client MIS reports that aren't asked for, read, or indeed needed. They didn't use half of the ones we were producing in the US, so we stopped producing them. It has reduced our MIS costs by 22.7 % and our clients have responded very positively. Maybe this is something you could all do too?" JR looked proud of himself.

Samuel sat up straight and looked coldly at JR: "*I* didn't know you'd done that. That may impact *my* clients. Have you stopped them globally or just in the US?"

"But I *did* send an email to everyone, informing you of this. And yes, it's global."

Christine said: "Yes, you asked me to stop them, so I did. I saw the email".

"I did *not* see any email. Why didn't you tell me, Christine? You're in charge of MIS; I would expect you to let me know". Samuel stared accusingly at Christine.

"Why do I need to send another email, when JR had already sent an email? I assumed you knew. Why didn't you read JR's email?"

"I get so many emails and if I've only been copied in, I assume it's for information purposes only and not something major".

"I'm sure I didn't just copy you in, I would have addressed it to you too" JR retorted in a defensive way.

"Well, I'm sure you didn't or I would have read it. So when we lost that very important, highly profitable customer last week, it was your fault. Now I understand. That must have been the final straw that made them leave us, after all the other challenges they'd had after the merger. This is the first significant customer that we've lost so far." Samuel crossed his arms, and leaned back.

So far Stephen had been quiet, listening to the others' conversation.

And now the penny dropped. This is what had been bothering him all day. He had known something wasn't quite right. The global client they had lost the previous week, a highly profitable one, had been affected by his group's lack of communication and ownership alongside their unclear roles. He was horrified. His team was not working together at all; they were just existing next to one another!

"This is not good" he said. "I think you're right we've really screwed up on this one. I have a meeting with Helmut next week and I know that this is one of the things he wants to talk about. We really need to figure out what happened, what errors were made. This must not happen again".

As Stephen tried to compose himself, Christine burst out: "Why are you all blaming me? You should be working with each other, communicating more. It's not my fault. I have other problems, I don't' need this." Her voice rose and became shaky. As the others watched her they were startled to see her start sobbing. She left the table abruptly. It had happened so quickly, one minute they were talking about the customer issue, the next Christine accused them of blaming her and now she was in tears.

It had become really chilly now. The group fell silent and Stephen said: "Let's talk about this at breakfast. It's late anyway. I'll go and see if Christine is OK".

"Do you want me to go and talk to her?" Sophia asked. Stephen hesitated and then, in a relieved voice, said: "Yes, if you wouldn't mind. That might be better".

Sophia left and the others were unsure of what to say or do next. They were all uncomfortable by the sudden outburst of emotion that had interrupted the otherwise light-hearted evening. They sat staring at anything but each other, looking for some inspiration in their drinks or on the floor. JR was gazing into the distance.

Christine was sitting in an armchair in the corner of an empty lounge at the front of the house, overlooking the drive. The crying had stopped and she sat quietly, reflecting, her face drawn and pale. As Sophia got near, Christine looked up but didn't say anything.

"Are you OK?" Sophia asked softly.

"Yeah, I'm fine... I guess. There's been a lot going on lately. I shouldn't let my personal life come into work though. But I guess I just did".

"Do you want to talk about it?" Sophia queried.

"No, not really. But I should probably say something to you all. It was really unlike me to explode like that." She paused.

"I'm getting a divorce, you see. We've been married for six years and have been on a trial separation for the last 3 months, and now I've just found out that my husband wants to make the separation permanent. I've been getting some emails from him today. Not a good way to let someone know."

Sophia nodded "Oh Christine, I'm really sorry. Can I do anything to help?"

"Let's go back to the others. I want to get this over with and tell them now."

She stood up, straightened her back and took a deep breath. It was suddenly becoming very real to her, having said it out loud. In some strange kind of way, it made her feel stronger.

They headed back out onto the terrace, where the others were quietly discussing football results. They looked up and went quiet as Christine and Sophia appeared.

Stephen's Journal

What a day it's been! I can't sleep. So many things seemed to happen today.

I think the thing I'm most upset about is how the lack of teamwork in my team seems to have led to the loss of this important client. How did I let this happen? What's my role in this? I'm not sure the team building has resolved the issues that created this situation.

The afternoon was great though; I had a true glimmer of hope of what this team could be. There was a sense of camaraderie and drive that I liked. It feels like we all know each other a bit better now. I do realise that it is not enough to solve the issues that were revealed today though. We need to do more to make this a good and effective team. The team seems to have bonded and I'm certain we can build on this somehow. To be honest, I think we need to spend some more time together, the whole team.

Leading this team is actually harder than I thought it would be. I know I just want it all to work, for people to get on and do their jobs, but it's not quite that simple, I recognise that now. I need some help. But from where?

And then there's Christine. What on earth?! I had no idea all of that was going on. How did I miss it? Alice always tells me I should pick up more on what's going on with people and the dynamics of people, but I find it quite hard. Or maybe it's just that I haven't focused much on it so far? Oh! Now that I think about it, I did see that Christine was hanging back on her quad bike, but I disregarded it as I was so busy with the race. Hm. What could I have done differently? I certainly didn't know what to do when she had that outburst at dinner. And I was relieved when Sophia offered to talk to Christine, as I didn't know what to do, it felt so personal.

Samuel ducking out of the quad bikes has made me wonder if he really wants to be a part of this team. Is he going to hold us back? I should have talked to him today, but there just didn't seem to be a good moment. He had a point though, about how JR could have done more to make sure everyone was informed. We all have a part in this.

I so need to get this team working well. I'm off to see Helmut next week and he'll ask me some tough questions, that's for sure.

On a personal note, Christine has made me realise how much I appreciate Alice and that I need to consider my work/life balance. Oh, I have a lot to think about... then to do something about! But first, some sleep.

Chapter 5: The Agreement

"Teamwork doesn't tolerate the inconvenience of distance."

Unknown

The following morning breakfast was served in the big, sunny dining room. The room had high ceilings and whitewashed walls with huge windows on three of the four sides. The sun's bright rays had already made it warm. Each white dining room table was surrounded by 18th century chairs with traditional blue and white check woven covers. The breakfast sounds were faded out by the seagulls, which seemed to be having lively conversations with each other outside the window.

Over breakfast, the team picked up again on the subject of the customer they had lost. It wasn't an easy subject but they all knew it had to be done. They shared some ideas and decided to put in place some actions that would help them divide up tasks more clearly between team members, thus making sure this kind of thing didn't happen again. Up until then, it had all run smoothly.

"There's something else here as well, isn't there, about us as a team? Is there anything we need to do differently, as a *team*?" asked JR, emphasising the word team.

They had been focusing on the tasks and not really looking at their relationships with each other or the other dynamics that had been playing out in the team. JR was trying to get the team to think about this.

"There's one thing we can do for sure" started Anna. "It's clear that we don't all treat each others' emails as a priority. Could we put an agreement in place that says that all of us treat each others' emails as a priority? Just like we would if the email had come from one of our customers. Could we do that?" Anna paused. "The fact that we didn't really treat each other's emails as important was the real reason we lost that customer. I don't like that feeling".

Sophia nodded. "Yes that sounds like a great idea. Imagine what it would be like if we all really did treat each other like customers. It would make a huge difference. I have to agree, that's not how I currently view you". She looked at her colleagues with some embarrassment. "*What would it be like*", she thought, "*if I treated JR as a customer?*" Treating her peers as customers was a new concept and it seemed so obvious now. She was excited as she realised this could make all the difference to the team, and ultimately their external customers too.

She wasn't the only one who was having a moment of bright realisation. The room went quiet and Stephen could see some nods around the table. The new awareness that they did not view each other as customers was quite a revelation. They had simply not been seeing *this* team or its members as important.

Christine contributed: "What if we agree to respond to any email sent from a member of this team within 24 hours? Can we commit to that? Would 24 hours be OK?"

"I can't commit to that, I get far too many emails" said Samuel, shaking his head. "I can't commit to that", he repeated.

"I turn my emails around instantly. Sure we can do it. I suggest 12 hours. I would respond to my customer in 12 hours so I can happily commit to do the same for this team" JR replied.

"I agree with 24 hours"

"Me too"

"In fact if I'm going to treat you like a customer then, yeah me too"

"As the majority agree with 24 hours, that's what we'll do. So can we all commit to responding to each other's emails within 24 hours?" Stephen repeated this purposefully, emphasising the question. "Do I have your agreement as well, Samuel?"

Samuel slowly nodded his head, which meant agreement, but said nothing.

Stephen had now taken charge and gained everyone's commitment. He felt good.

There was a sense of progress in the team as they finally left for the airport, leaving the peaceful archipelago behind them.

*

Two weeks later the team members were reunited for a team conference call.

Stephen, Sophia and Christine were all seated around Stephen's desk with the phone in prime position. They were all focusing on it; their eyes fixated on its star-like shape and its speakers that sprawled out across the desk. The microphones were pushed out towards them like long tentacles.

It made a sound: "Beep beep"

"Who just joined?" asked Stephen, as the conference call kicked off.

"It's Anna here. Hi!"

"Hi Anna, have we got JR on the line too?" There was silence.

"OK, no JR yet"

"I'm here"

"Is that you, Samuel?"

"Yes".

"OK, so we're just missing JR. Let's get started, he can catch up"

"Beep beep" went the phone again.

"Hi guys, sorry I'm late. It's early here". It was JR. The team members were now all gathered.

"How's my quad bike racing partner today? I've been practicing so I'll really get you next time!"

Sophia giggled and retorted, in no uncertain terms, "We shall see about that".

Stephen noticed the healthy banter and was pleased about it, although he believed everything had a time and a place. Now it was time to get on with business. He didn't like small talk much and he considered this small talk.

Stephen's office was on the small side; a number of offices had been divided into smaller offices in order to fit in all of the employees in the new organisation. In his new office, he still had a window though and through this window, the sun was streaming in, hot and bright in the early afternoon hour. Stephen was just thinking that the blinds needed to come down, when Christine got up and pulled hard at the cord on the blinds, which fell with a loud thud. Stephen nodded his approval and gave her a small smile. As the sun shone through the gaps in the blind the dust particles danced in the air over the table.

"Let me take you through the agenda for this call. First I want to give you an update on my meeting with Helmut. Then I want you to give me an update on how you're progressing with your financials and the savings that we're looking for. Then we may have time for "any other business". Is there anything you'd like to add to the agenda?" Stephen paused.

There was a crackle on the line and Anna was waiting for a gap to give her input.

"I think we should talk about our recent team building".

"Yes, that's fine if we have time at the end. We'll see."

"So let me give you an update from Helmut".

The next 10 minutes were a monologue performed by Stephen. He liked this, he felt in charge when he was doing the talking. The message was clear from Helmut; the integration, the subsequent optimisation and the productivity rise expected as a result were taking too long. Helmut just wanted them to sort it out. There wasn't much direction, if any, on how this should be done; just turn the results around. As it had been a monologue from Stephen, the team members were unsure if they were being asked to respond, or whether they were even expected to respond.

The silence that followed was only interrupted by the tapping on a keyboard, coming from the speaker phone. Christine moved her head to one side tilting her ear towards the phone. *"Am I hearing that correctly?"* she thought.

JR spoke, interrupting her thoughts, "Is someone typing? If we're on a call, we're on a call". He sounded irritated.

The typing stopped. *"I should have called them on that"*, Stephen thought, belatedly.

"Hrm. Let's get on with the updates. Samuel, do you want to go first?"

"Sorry, what was that?" Samuel's voice was gruff.

Stephen rolled his eyes, catching himself as Christine noticed.

"I'd like you to start your update please, Samuel. Where are you with the numbers for your team?"

"I've reviewed my numbers and as I had expected, I've come to the conclusion that I am already running a tight ship and cannot really make any more improvements. So we'll just have to find the cost reductions elsewhere".

Christine almost shouted: "You're always going on about how good your team is, but when others ask you for help and advice, to share your *'fantastic'* experience, you don't respond! I'm starting to think that you're not really on the same team as us. I sent an email to all of you last week asking for your knowledge on a global customer and you're the only one who still hasn't responded. Everyone else responded in 24 hours, as we had agreed, but I've had nothing from you."

"I've been really busy".

That was all he said. His colleagues were surprised at his response. All eyes and ears were on Stephen now, what was he going to do about it? They had all agreed, it had been a *team* agreement, and if it was going to work then they were all going to have to stick to it.

The previously hot room suddenly felt cooler. The tension carried itself from the room, through the airwaves of the phone to each team member scattered around the globe.

"Yes, we all need to respect this agreement. To help us with this, does everyone get the 'team whereabouts' spreadsheet? Where we can all see where everyone is? For example, the one that I'm currently looking at shows that Samuel is working from home today. He should therefore be able to answer emails within the 24 hour deadline whereas next week, when Anna is on holiday, she won't be able to."

"But you're in the office today, Samuel!" Sophia exclaimed.

"W-w-what?" Stephen stuttered. "Are you in the office?"

"Yes, I am. Why?"

"If you're here then why didn't you join the call in my office, like everyone else?"

It was obvious to everyone that Stephen was beyond annoyed. The question on everyone's mind: what was he going to do about it? It was dawning on everyone that Samuel was there, in the office, and had made the decision not to join them in the room. He was actively distancing himself from them. They were all visualising him sitting close by, alone in his office.

"I didn't want to, it gets so crowded. It seemed to make more sense to just dial in."

The tension on the call got more intense; people seemed to be very still. The line crackled.

"OK, fine. Just let me know next time".

Anna was upset. She was the one who had been so excited about Stephen getting the job but now she was really beginning to doubt that his leadership was strong enough. She couldn't believe that he hadn't held Samuel accountable for his blatant disregard for their team agreement.

The call finished after a difficult, uncomfortable, and slightly disjointed round of updates. Whatever previous progress the team had achieved seemed to have been entirely undone.

Stephen's journal

Damn it! I'm so angry. I hardly know where to start!

What happened? What's wrong with Samuel? How is he making me look in front of the team? I don't know what to do about him. I know I should have done something today, but I just froze. I just didn't know what to do, again. Maybe I've just been very lucky so far in my career and just not had to deal with these kinds of problems? But I'm not a bad leader, I must be able to deal with this too. I know that I didn't want to have a bust-up on the call. I don't want to be seen to lose my temper. His arrogance just gets to me and gets in the way of me being a good leader. I know it's disruptive; it's affecting the team and the teamwork. Plus, it's making me really anxious, because what happens now? I can sense the team was disappointed and rightly so, I realise that. Wow, that's quite a realisation...but it doesn't feel good. Now what?

Alice would like that: the 'realisation'. Maybe she's right. Maybe I should talk to her? I need to talk to someone. I will talk to her!

I can see that this is affecting the teamwork, which in turn is affecting our productivity. I don't want Helmut to make that connection, and I certainly don't want him on my back about this. I need to sort it out. I need to address it, when I'm calmer.

I have some great people on the team, but I seem to focus all my attention on Samuel and the rest of the team is too. I have to change this.

Whatever I have done so far is not enough. Or maybe it would have been if I had stood up to Samuel today? I didn't though and it's time for me to take a long hard look at myself, and how I'm managing this team. I haven't done great so far, I confess.

Chapter 6: A Chance Meeting

"No-one is an island and everyone needs the help of others now and then. It's OK to ask for help."

Stephen and Alice were speeding down the motorway towards the south coast. Stephen's parents were celebrating their wedding anniversary and the whole family was invited. This break was entirely welcome; he had been looking forward to it for weeks. He finally had a chance to get away from the stresses and pressures of work. He also hadn't seen his sister for 6 months. He had spoken to his mum earlier in the week and apparently Emma had a new boyfriend who was also coming along. Stephen was curious; it was quite unusual for his sister to bring boyfriends to meet the family. Was this a special one?

He became aware of Alice looking at him. He turned to her and asked: "Excited about the weekend?"

"Yes, I am. I enjoy seeing your family. You looked deep in thought though. What were you thinking about? Not work I hope?"

"No, I wasn't actually. I was thinking about this new boyfriend of Emma's. Have you heard much about him? You talked to Emma last week."

"Yes, in fact, Emma mentioned that he's someone you know. It would appear that you went to school together."

"Who is he? Did you catch his name?"

"I don't know. I can't remember. I guess you'll find out when we see him tomorrow."

"Yeah, I guess."

"So what are we doing today?"

"Well, you and I are going out for dinner tonight as Mum and Dad are seeing some friends. So I've booked a table at this new restaurant. I think you'll like it. It'll be just you and me."

"Great!" Alice gazed out the window, smiling softly at the view of the South Downs; she never tired of the sight of the rolling countryside that was the Downs.

The South Downs chalk hills run along part of the south-east coast of England. Large parts of it are unpopulated, enticing outdoor enthusiasts of all kinds. The South Downs National Park is known as one of 'Britain's Breathing Spaces'. Anyone who has visited this area will recognise that description; she unconsciously took a deep breath.

Alice reminisced about how she and Stephen had walked the Downs, around Devil's Dyke, earlier that spring. It always surprised her how close to London all this wonderful landscape was, and how the undulating hills almost spilled into the sea. On that particular day, the clouds hung close to the hilltops but a bright gap was appearing in the sky between the Downs and the clouds. All of a sudden the whole landscape became brighter, the colours more intense.

Something caught Alice's eye high in the sky. A kite soared above; it caught the wind, floating on the thermals like a big, proud bird. Alice imagined what it would be like to float so freely above the green patchwork quilt landscape; high above the vivid colours, the emeralds, the moss greens. She thought about Stephen, things didn't seem to be going well with his team at the moment. Maybe this is what he needed? Perhaps he would benefit from an external perspective; someone flying above it all, who could see the whole 'landscape'?

With some reluctance she turned her attention back to the present.

"I'm glad you talked to me about what's happening for you at work. This is not the kind of thing you should have to worry about on your own. I know you don't want to talk about work now, but I've had another thought that I want to share with you. I've just read an article about the choices a leader has; to be reactive or proactive with their team. It also talks about the effect the choice has on their results. I don't remember the exact details of it though. It wasn't until afterwards that I thought about you and your team. I need to find that article again."

"Sounds interesting. I really want to find a solution".

"I have a good feeling about this weekend. Maybe you'll find some inspiration for this solution you're after? Getting away for a while can give you a fresh perspective; sometimes things just fall into place".

*

At breakfast the next morning, Stephen and Alice were enjoying their coffee, while Stephen's mum was updating them about all the relatives that were coming to today's celebration. There were names that Stephen barely recognised, people he hadn't seen for years. The party was to be held at a country house, a few miles further inland.

"Emma and Gerry will be here in an hour. Then, we'll all head off to the party together."

"Gerry? You don't mean Gerry Robertson, do you?"

"I sure do. You haven't seen him for a long time, have you? You and Gerry used to have so much fun; you were great friends. What happened? Did you just lose touch?"

"Yes, I haven't seen him for at least 10 years. I wonder what he's been up to. I seem to remember he went to New York with some bank. So he's back. Great! I can't wait to see him. Go Emma!"

"Well don't forget you have a lot of cousins you haven't seen in a long time too. Make sure you don't just spend the whole day talking to Gerry".

"Yes, Mum" Stephen smiled, thinking *"some things never change"*.

*

Gerry was just as Stephen remembered him: jovial, friendly, talkative and just a really likeable guy. Furthermore, he was successful. Over the course of the afternoon they caught up on the lost years and Stephen became aware that Gerry had done really well for himself. After 4 years in New York, he now had a senior position in the City, leading a new, global team; a bit like Stephen himself but with a much larger team, a whole division in fact.

The party was in full swing around them; smiling, happy people were sipping drinks at the anniversary reception. Soft piano music surrounded them and the double doors leading to the garden were wide open. Through the doors, the white peacocks were looking beautiful, wandering aimlessly around the ornate lawn in the warm afternoon sunshine. They had kept away from the hotel and were circling at a safe distance.

"So Gerry, how are you enjoying being back home, in good old England?" Alice smiled at Gerry. She and Emma had just joined the guys in the drawing room.

"I loved working in New York, it was great, a really good experience. I enjoyed living in the States, and what's not to like about New York?" The others nodded their agreement. "I am happy to be back though, especially now I've met Emma again". He squeezed her hand and she winked back at him.

"I hear you're in London too. What are you up to?" It was Gerry's turn to be inquisitive.

"I'm currently in the aftermath of a merger; one that's proving more challenging than I thought. It's interesting in some ways, but I had no idea the number of people issues I was going to face. Anyway, let's not focus on that, not today".

"Oh, I know all about people issues. My current team has had a rocky journey, but we have finally turned the corner and I can't tell you how relieved I am! It's had a tremendous impact on the business as well. I might just get a bonus this year. I could be laughing all the way to the bank!"

Overcoming his initial reluctance to talk business, Stephen was intrigued: "What happened? What did you do?"

At that moment, lunch was announced and the group was ushered into the dining room. They agreed to continue the conversation later.

On the way to their seats, Alice said: "It sounds like Gerry might have some experience that you can benefit from. Do you feel OK talking to him about your issues with your team?

I know you didn't want to talk about work, but this might just be too good to miss?"

"I like and trust Gerry, I always did. I don't really have anyone else I can talk to anyway, so yeah, why not".

"Good, that's settled then. So when we've finished eating, let's catch him!"

*

Late in the evening, with cognacs in hand, the four friends were reunited in the library. Stephen had talked to a multitude of cousins, second-cousins, aunts and uncles and could retire to the library, guilt free.

"I love summer. There's something very optimistic about summer" Emma rested her head on the back of her winged armchair, kicked off her shoes and curled her legs underneath her. The warm summer evening drifted in from the outside.

"Gerry, what happened with your team? Tell us about it."

"Oh yes, my team. Well, I inherited a team with a lot of baggage. I don't know how my predecessor had worked with them but when I joined, you couldn't really even call them a 'team'. They were all working on their own thing. They didn't spend any time together and they didn't want to. In fact, I'd go as far as saying that rather than working together, they were pretty much working against each other; all fighting their own corner. And it felt like fighting! Needless to say, they didn't welcome me with open arms. What was worse is that as I realised the severity of the team's problems, it made me question my own ability as a leader to resolve the situation."

As Gerry opened up, the atmosphere felt more intense, closer somehow. Without even thinking, Stephen, Emma and Alice had moved forward slightly, leaning in to take in more of the story.

"Really? I didn't know you felt like that." Emma looked sad.

"I don't feel like that now, but I did."

"What happened?" asked Stephen eagerly, thinking how much this could help him.

"Well. I won't bore you with my initial failings, because believe you me, there were quite a few! Then something happened and I realised that I could make different choices as a leader. I hadn't considered those choices." Gerry grinned.

"Wait a minute!" Alice exclaimed, "That sounds like the article I read, about the 2 choices of a leader. Is that what you are talking about Gerry?"

"Indeed. I know exactly the article you are talking about, and that's how I created the success for the team."

They were all excited now, hanging on his every word.

"How did you do it?"

"From that article, I was able to track someone down who told me what I needed to do to create a really powerful team that worked effectively together, alongside me as their leader. I learned how to create a vision with the team; a compelling reason for the team to be together. They had never had that and they were a part of creating it too. So rather than having to drag my team along, it taught me how to bring my team with me because *they* wanted to." Gerry paused.

"Did you learn anything about what to do if someone breaks an agreement you've made as a team?"

"In what way, what do you mean?"

"Well, let me give you an example. We agreed, as a team, that we would reply to each others' emails within 24 hours, unless on holiday or away. Then one of the team members blatantly disregarded this in front of everyone, including me. What's more, he didn't seem to think it was a problem. And I didn't do anything." Stephen startled himself with this confession.

As they were sitting there, in that friendly environment, comfortable and safe, Stephen actually felt OK about opening up. It was almost cathartic.

"No-one else said anything either. What do you think I should have done? This has really been playing on my mind." Stephen went quiet.

"I had a real 'aha' moment about holding people to account, and the level of trust you need to have within the team to be able to do that. Agreements need to be made at a behavioural and emotional level, not just an action and task level. That's what needs to happen, but your 24 hour email example was at an action and task level, which doesn't gain real buy-in emotionally. So perhaps your team members don't feel compelled to hold each other to account?" Gerry raised his eyebrows in question.

"I don't quite get it. How could I have made that team agreement behavioural? Surely responding within 24 hours is a behaviour?"

"Yes, but you need to have a much deeper discussion and agreement within the team about acceptable and non-acceptable behaviours, and their impact on team success. The team must really make the link that these behaviours *are* how the team achieves success. Everybody needs to care enough about the commitments to the team, to then hold each other accountable in a supportive and respectful way."

Gerry looked at the others, realising it was probably getting too late for this kind of discussion. He concluded:

"Guys, I could talk about this for hours. This was just *one* of my 'learnings', I've got loads more to share, but I think we should call it a night. It's getting late and we are at a family function after all. We'd better go and mingle with all your cousins!" Gerry nudged Emma playfully.

"This has been a real eye-opener, Gerry. I need some more information for sure. Can you please send me the details of the people you worked with?" Alice was amazed at how energetic Stephen looked. She hadn't seen him like this for a long time.

"Sure, Stephen. Let's catch up on Monday."

Stephen's journal

Wow! What a weekend!

Alice was right. Sometimes just getting away makes things clearer. What Gerry said about team agreements actually really made sense. Not sure how to do it, but the idea is fascinating.

She was right about how I needed to talk to someone. I've kept all this to myself for too long. It felt liberating to talk to an old, trusted friend. I trust and respect Gerry and that made the difference. I think it also made us feel closer again; it was as if it had only been a few weeks since we last met. Amazing that it's been over 10 years!

Things seem clearer. I am going to take action on this; I will call Gerry on Monday and get the details. The time has come to deal with Samuel; no more beating around the bush.

Chapter 7: The team 'talks' without Stephen

"We must all hang together, or assuredly, we shall all hang separately."

Benjamin Franklin

Subject: Confidential

Hi Sophia

Good to talk the other day. I needed to speak to someone in the team about what happened in that call and you're the only one I trust. I hope you don't mind me contacting you.

Can you believe Stephen didn't say anything to Samuel about him not honouring our 24 hour email commitment? Maybe the archipelago was a waste of time! I don't want to sound negative, but I don't think this is going in the right direction at all. And what about that customer thing? I think it's pretty obvious that it was Samuel's fault we lost that customer. Helmut's really not happy about what happened, he wants to get to the bottom of it all, he wants someone to blame. I wonder if he knows what happened. Do you think Stephen has told him?

What can we do about all of this?

I really don't need this right now, I have so much else to think about. We've started the divorce proceedings... Help!

Sorry,
Christine

Subject: Re: Confidential

Hi Christine

Of course you can talk to me. I'm sorry to hear about the divorce. I know it's a cliché, but it'll get better, I promise. Hang in there. Let me know if I can help, really, I mean it.

About the work thing: I think Stephen is doing the best he can. I agree that he should have done something different in the call, but it just didn't happen. All we can do is to maybe give him the feedback?

I thought the archipelago was good. I just think we need to do some more work on us becoming a proper team, not a team in name alone. We need to talk about these things, but there's never time for it in our calls, and we so rarely meet. We should talk to Stephen about this, we definitely should.

Regarding the customer issue, I don't think we should be telling Helmut anything. We need to leave that to Stephen and trust that he does what he's supposed to be doing.

Apart from that, I'm not sure what we can do. I'll have a think about it.

Take care,
Sophia

Subject: For your eyes only

Hi JR

How's my racing partner? :-)

I hear you've got a heat wave over in NY. I envy you; it's raining here in London (I know what you're thinking, but we've had a lot of sun this summer too!).

What did you think about that last team call? Can you believe Samuel was in the office, yet didn't join us in Stephen's room where we were all dialled in! Not to mention the fact that he didn't join in the quad biking, or respond within 24 hours as agreed. I don't get him; it's as if he wants us to fail. That can't be true, can it? And what about him accusing you of losing that customer? That was quite unfair, I think.

What do you think is going on in the team, and what should we do? Maybe we could have a chat later in the week?

Thanks
Sophia

Subject: Re: For your eyes only

Hi Sophia

I'm fine, thank you, and ready for another race whenever you dare ☺

I'm not surprised Samuel didn't bother to turn up in the room. I really don't trust him. If truth be told, I think we have a major trust issue in the team, which is certainly not helping us do our jobs. I think he has his own hidden agenda, and I want to figure out what it is. I think Samuel is talking to Helmut, I'm not sure, but I heard something. I don't like spreading rumours so I won't say anything else for the moment; I'd rather wait until I know more. Hope you understand.

Stephen is over here next week for a review. I may just need to talk to him then.

Let's touch base soon
JR

Subject: Confidential – book a call

Herr Helmut Greisend,

I'm contacting you to let you know that I have some concerns about the leadership of our team, and I think you, as our senior leader, need to know. Can I please book a call with you as soon as possible to discuss this? It is important that we talk soon, as I believe this may shine a light on the recent customer issue that I know you are aware of.

I await your response.

Yours sincerely,

Samuel Stone

Stephen's Journal

That call with Gerry today really helped clarify a few more things. I'm starting to understand what I need to do. I feel good.

I know I need to get the team back together again. We need to increase the trust level within the team, that's our number one priority. I've also become conscious that we need to work much more on HOW we make this team successful, not just WHAT we do to create success (which frankly, we currently aren't!)

I'll pick it up with JR next week. He seems like a good guy.

Chapter 8: A Manhattan dinner reveals an unpleasant truth

"You need to show trust to get trust."

Stephen relaxed back into his seat. The Boeing 747 had reached its cruising height and was now gliding smoothly through the air. The sun shone brightly in through his window, high above the clouds that he had left behind in London. He sipped his Coke, revelling in the respite from everything. He had intended to work, but the list of films was too tempting; he gave in.

Three films later he landed at JFK Airport on Long Island, NY. It felt good to stretch his legs again and after the traditional wait at immigration, he collected his luggage amongst the many, noisy tourists. The airport was a hive of activity; people trying to control unruly luggage carts, find children and bags that they could have sworn were there a minute ago, looking around for signs: the toilets, the exit. Bag in hand, Stephen headed for the doors. Swerving to avoid a group of laughing women, he shot past. Finally free of the crowd! He hastened towards the exit. The heat hit him like a sticky, humid wall when the sliding doors parted. At last, he escaped the terminal building.

"Damn hot today" his cab driver said a few minutes later. *"You've got that right"*, thought Stephen, sweltering in the back of the taxi. The air con in the cab wasn't working so he had the windows rolled down to their maximum, all the way into Manhattan. JR had said it was hot in New York at the moment, but Stephen hadn't quite expected this.

New York always invigorated him. He envied Gerry for having lived in this vibrant, buzzing city that never slept. He wondered what it would be like to live here. He thought about where Gerry had lived, he had mentioned something about the Upper West side. His thoughts were drifting and before he knew it, the taxi had pulled up outside his hotel.

After having checked in, and taken a quick refreshing shower, he went for a walk. As he strolled down the street he took out his phone and called JR, reaching only his answer phone:

"Hi JR. It's Stephen. Just to let you know that I'm here. I've just arrived at my hotel. Call me when you get this message so we can meet up later this afternoon, or maybe even for an early dinner. I'm on my mobile, my cell. Thanks". He hung up and headed for Starbucks; a coffee would give him the injection of caffeine that would help fight off some of the jetlag.

*

JR listened to Stephen's message. He sighed. There were things happening in the team that Stephen was oblivious to. JR knew he had to be the one to enlighten him; he just didn't have it in him to conceal the truth. It wasn't something he was looking forward to though. He needed to think through how he was going to tell Stephen at dinner.

His thoughts were racing; like the powerboat that, in the corner of his eye, roared by on the Hudson River. His office was small but it had that coveted window view. The river was busy, as always, and he noticed the Hoboken ferry leaving the World Financial Center terminal. He glanced at his watch, aware that the first afternoon ferry left shortly after 3.30pm. His watch confirmed that it was, indeed, already that late in the afternoon. He found it hard to concentrate. He started pacing up and down but then forced himself to sit down again; he was running out of time.

After his initial email contact with Sophia, things had gotten a whole lot worse. Samuel had called JR out of the blue, apparently to talk about what a poor leader Stephen was. JR had not been sure what he was after, why he had called. It felt like Samuel was just bad-mouthing Stephen. Of course, JR hadn't shared his view and had said to Samuel that he should talk to Stephen directly if he had an issue with him. The following day Sophia informed him that Samuel had called the entire team, one by one, to talk about Stephen. It was a web of deceit, and Samuel was the spider.

As if that wasn't enough, Helmut had been in NY the same week and had cornered JR after a meeting, asking him outright about Stephen's leadership: "I've heard from Samuel that Stephen's lack of leadership cost us a valuable customer. Is this right? What can *you* tell me about Stephen's leadership?" The directness of Helmut's question had startled JR greatly.

He took a deep breath. It was simple, he just had to tell Stephen the whole story and it needed to be done today. JR picked up the phone to return Stephen's call.

*

Stephen had found a table outside a trendy restaurant in the Meatpacking District. JR had suggested it for dinner and Stephen was impressed with the colonial style décor. The smells from the kitchen were spicy and promising. It brought back memories of Asian holidays with Alice. He sat and watched the world go by, tired and relaxed in equal parts, his thoughts wandering. All of a sudden a shadow fell across the table, bringing him back down to earth. JR had appeared in front of him.

"Hi, welcome to New York! Had a good trip?"

Stephen got up and shook his hand. "Yes, thanks. Looks like a great choice of restaurant."

"Yeah, I come here a lot, I like it. Have you checked out the menu?"

"Yes, I must admit I've been eyeing it up since I got here. I'm starving. Let's order."

Over dinner, JR took the opportunity to update Stephen on some of the usual work related subjects: headcount, service levels, customer challenges that he needed to be aware of. He was wondering when the right moment would come up to talk about Samuel.

When coffee arrived, Stephen said: "I want to talk to you about the team. I think we need to do some more work together on our team development, on how we work together. I was contemplating getting someone in to facilitate a team session for us. We're too focused on *what* we do, the tasks and transactions. We need to balance our focus by also considering *how* we do things, our impact on the world around us. I wanted to talk it through with you".

JR hesitated, the moment had come, he realised. Now was his opportunity to tell Stephen what had happened. He was apprehensive, but ploughed on just the same. He felt a sense of responsibility, especially based on what Stephen had just said. It had to be now.

JR cleared his throat. "Before we talk about that, there's something you should know."

Stephen put down his glass, and sat back in his chair. The tone of JR's voice inferred this was serious. He looked at JR with curiosity and gave the tiniest hint of a nod, meaning 'continue'.

"Samuel is talking about you behind your back. He's talked to everyone in the team, and to Helmut, about your leadership", JR blurted out.

"He did what?" Stephen could feel his face turning red with anger. He couldn't believe what he'd just heard.

"Yes, there's no easy way of saying this so I will just tell you exactly what happened. I don't want to go behind your back". This was followed by a questioning glance at Stephen, for approval to carry on.

Stephen's thoughts were flying around in his head. He forced himself to take a deep breath and just listen. He shrugged, indicating it was OK for JR to go on.

"There's been some concern, within in the team, about the state of the team. We were all a bit disappointed about how you handled Samuel's non-compliance with our email rule. Samuel has contacted Helmut; I heard it from Helmut himself". At this Stephen put his hand to his head. JR continued, "He told him that your lack of leadership was the reason we lost that customer. Helmut asked me what I thought. I want you to know that *I* supported you." He lowered his voice.

Stephen stared in disbelief, "*the nerve of that Samuel! I should have done something about this before*". He quietly berated himself and took a big gulp of coffee.

"That's not all. Samuel has also been soliciting views from everyone on the team regarding your leadership. First I thought he had only talked to me, but Sophia let me know that she and all the others had been contacted too. I'm not quite sure what he's trying to achieve, but I get the sense he is working to turn the team against you. This has now gone too far, you need to deal with it. You started talking about a team session, but frankly I don't think a team session will solve this. You need to resolve this situation with Samuel first. After that we can go on to build the team."

The honesty of JR's words made Stephen feel embarrassed. He had a sinking feeling in his stomach. He didn't say anything and JR didn't rush him; he realised that Stephen needed a moment to reflect on what had been said.

JR was relieved that it was all said and he hoped that Stephen would appreciate his positive intent.

After what seemed like an eternity, Stephen responded. "Thank you. I'm really grateful that you told me. I know it can't have been easy. I need to think about what to do, but you can trust that I will take care of this". He paused, "It's getting late and I'm tired, let's get the bill, check, whatever you call it!"

"Sure" JR gestured at the waiter.

A couple of minutes later, they left. It was busy now; people were spilling from the pavement into the road. The evening was warm and the air full of laughter.

JR flagged down a cab, while Stephen decided to walk back to his hotel. They said their goodbyes.

As Stephen was walking, he was uttering expletives under his breath. He was angry, fearful and questioning himself wildly:

"Why did I let this get out of hand? What does Helmut think of me now? What did Samuel say to Helmut? How can I redeem myself? What am I going to do? I need to get back into control of this situation, I don't like this feeling. I feel out of control, as if this thing has taken on its own life!"

As he neared his hotel, he had already started to calm down. He racked his brain for something good to take from the situation he was in. The door swung open into his cool, air-conditioned room. As the coolness of the room hit him, it also hit him that the one good thing, one very good thing, was JR's courage to speak up. He was much better off knowing, than not knowing.

Stephen's Journal

I really respect JR for telling me everything straight up, as it is. Someone once told me that feedback is a gift. I always thought that sounded a bit stupid, but now I know what they mean. If he hadn't told me, I'd be flying blind. At least now I know, so I can prepare and take action.   Thank you, JR!

I also believe him when he said he supported me in front of Helmut. It's good to know that I have some support within the team. I wonder where the others are with this.

OK. Think Stephen, think. How do I best approach Samuel? Because I will approach him, that's for sure. I will.

Chapter 9: The Article

"There will be no fairy godmother with a magic wand, to wave your problems away. Stop sticking your head in the sand."

Stephen put his key in the lock and turned it with a sigh of relief. He was home. The flight back from New York had been an uncomfortable one; thoughts of his discussion with JR had been turning in his head all night. Alice had gone to work early, but had left him a note on top of an open magazine on the kitchen table, next to a coffee thermos. Smiling, he poured himself a cup and started reading.

Good morning globetrotter! Good to have you back home. I've found that article Gerry and I both talked about. Read it!

See you tonight, A xx

The Team Formula

What you're about to read will be straight-talk. This is not your typical management speak, because frankly we're tired of it. It hinders more than it helps. Worn-out clichés turn people off and take them off track.

So this is our straight-talk about teams. We're here to tempt you, to entice you to do something different to what most people do.

As a leader you have two choices. Your choice will make the difference between a poor, or even mediocre team, and an excellent one. What choice are you currently making as a leader?

<u>Choice 1</u>

You don't do anything in particular with your team, other than divide up tasks and provide them with physical equipment. Maybe you're thinking or saying something like this:

    a. We're all grown-ups here, so we all know what we're doing.
    b. You get paid to do your job, so just get on with it.
    c. I shouldn't have to tell intelligent people how to do their jobs.
    d. I'm so busy getting the job done. I can't handhold people, they must take responsibility themselves.

Choice 2

You actively work with your team, on <u>how</u> you work as a team. This does not need to be complicated.

So this is the simple team formula that will take you through the changing maze of teams. You get together as a team, you talk to each other, really talk to each other. You decide how to work together. You make a promise to each other, and you keep that promise. Most importantly, you get to know and trust each other. There it is.

Stephen stopped reading and sipped his coffee, which was cooling down. The rain smattered angrily against the window.

"Is it really that simple? Isn't it too simple?" He thought.

"What have I been doing with my team? Didn't we do all this in the archipelago? No, maybe we didn't. I know we talked about roles and responsibilities, but maybe that isn't enough".

He reflected further.

*"You know what? I think this just might work with my team! As a matter of fact, now that I think about it, it **was** that simple with JR; we just talked but I feel like we trust each other more. This is what I need to do with Samuel; just sit down and talk to him, really talk to him. Hmm. Food for thought".*

His eyes were drawn back to the article.

You could just leave it to chance and dumb luck. If you're lucky that may work. It's rare, but it has happened. So if you want to leave it to dumb luck, then good luck, you will need it!

If, on the other hand, you are different and are ready to make the first move, if you want to create a more engaged, successful team, a team that thrives even in challenging times, a remarkable team that gets the best results, then we congratulate you, you will be successful.

Maybe you are one of many leaders who are tired of:

- **Team members who don't know or trust each other**
- **Conflicts or tensions within the team**

- People who are not engaged, or maybe even apathetic about work
- A team that's not delivering as wanted or expected
- A team that's not well perceived by others
- People who are working in silos
- Everyone for themselves, fighting their own corner
- People who don't share relevant information with each other
- Cliques, sub-groups, teams within teams, "us and them" behaviours, gossiping and going behind people's backs.

If you're facing any of these problems, then listen up!

There will be no fairy godmother with a magic wand, to wave your problems away. Stop sticking your head in the sand. Don't run away to another team thinking it will be different. It rarely is.

So, are you ready for choice number 2?

Then here's more of the team formula. Here are some of the things you want to think about as the leader of a team, together with some subjects to discuss with the team:

- What's the purpose of the team? What's your compelling reason to work together? Do you need to be a team? If so, why?
- How well do people know and trust each other? How can you improve this level of familiarity and trust?

- How is the team perceived? How do you want to be perceived? How will you close that gap?
- How will you measure your success as a team? How will this success be achieved?
- How will you operate as a team? How will you spend your time together?
- Is the team problem-focused? How can you create solution-focus?
- Is the team proactive? Is it in charge of creating its own success?
- How motivated are the team members? Are they full of self esteem, confidence and drive?
- What behaviours are acceptable and unacceptable? How do you hold each other accountable for these promises? How do you make the team members understand the impact of their behaviours?
- Do you need help to guide the team through this process? (Not all leaders are effective facilitators, and that's OK, give yourself the permission to ask for help)

Every team finds themselves in a maze; a maze of rules and regulations, infrastructure and day-to-day demands, which change on a regular basis.

Rather than being stuck in this maze, or getting lost, this team formula helps you find the way through the maze. Everytime.

Just like people, teams are unique. Every team is different. Each team's challenges and contributions are surprisingly unique. As a result, the route is different for each team but the team formula is there to help you and the team figure out your unique roadmap. You find that you can't get through the maze on your own. You need the collective intelligence, experience, ideas and drive of the whole team to get there. That's when things happen.

One final thought. As a leader you need to believe that this will work (not just intellectually, but actually feel it in your gut), because what you believe with conviction drives your actions and results. If you believe with conviction, so will the team, and then you will get there.

Are *you* ready to make a move? Let's go.

Straight-talkers Mandy Flint and Elisabet Vinberg Hearn have guided teams through the maze for 30 years.

Stephen's Journal

What a great chat I had with Gerry today! Reading that article triggered something in me and I just had to call him.

Gerry agrees that it is as simple as that, that you really have to believe it and that it really works. It's had a huge impact on his team. Although at first, the team wasn't used to talking so freely and openly and honestly. Apparently, Gerry had to show the way by opening up himself, showing that he was ready to be vulnerable in order for others to trust him and feel safe.

I can be vulnerable. I'm going to have to be!

I've got to stop sticking my head in the sand and admit that I've been avoiding the difficult conversations, like the one I need to have with Samuel. Now. Or at least tomorrow! First some sleep.

Chapter 10: Stephen confronts Samuel

"Change is always possible. It's enough for one person to do something differently for change to happen."

Samuel strode into Stephen's office, a slight smirk on his face.

"Please take a seat" Stephen said formally, pointing to a chair opposite his own.

As Samuel settled into his chair, he nodded to the picture on Stephen's wall: "Picasso is nice, but not as a poster. You should have something more in keeping with the BS standard, now that we are all part of BS. They have a notable art collection, you know. Maybe it's time for you to learn a little bit more about art. I have a great knowledge of…"

Stephen interrupted him impatiently. He got straight to the point: "Look, I really want to talk to you. I know that you've talked to Helmut and the rest of my team about me. I would like to hear what you have to say."

Stephen felt relieved that he'd started, and now he just needed to stay calm and wait for Samuel's response. He studied Samuel closely. Alice had told him to not just listen, but also to watch for the unspoken messages in body language and mood.

Samuel seemed to be inspecting the nails on his right hand, before slowly putting his hand down and gazing blankly somewhere above Stephen's head.

"Well, there are some things about your leadership that simply needed to be said." Samuel declared unapologetically.

Stephen hadn't expected that bluntness. He was surprised that Samuel seemed so unremorseful when confronted.

"If you had a problem with my leadership, then why didn't you come straight to me?" Stephen retorted. He could feel the frustration grow and hoped it didn't show.

Samuel was very still, looking down. Stephen found it hard to read him, especially as he could not see his eyes.

"I just want you to be honest with me. What is it that you have a problem with?" Stephen forced himself to be quiet after that and allow Samuel to talk.

The silence was accentuated by the ping of an email coming from the laptop. Stephen waited. What was probably only seconds seemed like minutes.

Finally Samuel looked up and cleared his throat. He had obviously thought about how he was going to respond, knowing for a while that he would come to this crossroad. He sighed.

"I don't think you've taken your job seriously. What was all that quad-biking about? It was a complete waste of time. We are intelligent, experienced leaders – well most of us anyway – we should just all get on with running our own areas. I can do my job perfectly well without being part of this team; I don't need anyone in the team. In fact, it's as if you're asking us to run the team, and if that's the case, what is your role? I'm sure the others think the same."

"What are you trying to say?"

"Isn't it pretty obvious? I think you've got your focus wrong. I know all about leadership; it's about directing and telling people what to do. What you're doing is just confusing and it's certainly not helping the team."

"Leadership is so much more than that. What I'm trying to do is get us to work together, as a team, so that we can survive in this chaotic climate. I think we need each other and I don't think we can afford to work in silos, individually. I don't think I'd be doing my job if I wasn't trying to get the team together". Stephen was trying not to sound defensive, and at the same time, he started to feel more confident. He knew what he had done so far, although not really successful, had still been the right thing to do. This realisation made him feel even more assertive.

"I heard you told Helmut that it was my fault we lost that customer, you know which one I mean. Why did you do that? That's simply not true". Stephen was getting used to the direct approach.

Samuel looked away and said: "Well, it wasn't quite like that..." He trailed off.

Stephen jolted forward and spat out: "What was it like then?"

"Well, Helmut just asked me what happened. So I gave him my views on the handling of the customer screw-up. If you had done your job and made sure everyone was informed of important issues, this would never have happened."

"Samuel, you all need to take responsibility and talk to your colleagues. I can't be there every step of the way. This is exactly why you can't just do your own thing, you have to co-operate with each other. That's the whole reason why we have to work as a team, so these things don't happen again. You all think you can manage on your own, I say that's impossible. We must work together and I hope you can accept that, because that is the way it's going to have to be. "

Samuel didn't respond.

"I know how you like to think about things, so maybe you want to go away and reflect on that."

Stephen, making it clear that the conversation was over, got up from his swivel chair. He felt surprisingly calm and was confident that he was showing Samuel respect, even though he hadn't been granted the same respect.

Perversely, Stephen was now showing the kind of directive leadership that Samuel had wanted, but Samuel didn't like it and muttered something under his breath as he left.

Stephen's Journal

I wonder what will happen now.

Confronting Samuel was easier than I thought it would be. In fact, to be honest, the hardest part of the meeting was being quiet long enough to encourage Samuel to talk.

I got more out of this than I thought I would. I got myself ready for some straight talking with Samuel, but I hadn't expected, in return, to get the learning from him that I actually got. I now see that what I've done could have been potentially confusing to the team, so it's going to be more important than ever to spend time up front getting the team together and aligned. I also learned something about how I am perceived by others, well at least by Samuel. I'd quite like to know more about that. Scary thought, but perhaps I should talk to the other members of the team and ask for their perception of me too?

Alice had asked me to look for non-verbal communication but I don't find it easy, I think I need to do some more work on that. My gut feeling is that Samuel wasn't entirely open, but I might just be imagining that. Maybe I'm getting paranoid? In any case, I will keep my eye on Samuel.

Chapter 11: Everyone gets a call

"As a leader you have two choices and your choice will make the difference between a poor or even mediocre team, and an excellent one. What choice are you making as a leader?"

Seated in front of her computer, Sophia started up her email system and re-opened the email entitled 'Team Offsite no. 2', which she had read the day before.

Dear Team,

Further to our team meeting last week, I wanted to confirm the next steps in preparation for our team session.

Laura Firhaven from Amaziteam will contact each of you over the next few days to book an interview. The interviews are part of a Team Climate Study that Laura will perform for us. The purpose of this study is to get a clear picture of how this team is working. The focus will be on how we are working (behaviours, teamwork and relationships), rather than tasks and processes. It is a completely confidential process so please be open and honest with your responses.

The interview will take about 30 minutes.

In the team session, we will analyse the outcome of the study together in order to identify strengths, gaps, and how we need to work together to be as successful as possible. Laura will facilitate this session for us.

If you have any questions, please let me know.

Regards

Stephen

Bang on schedule, Sophia's phone rang at 10.00 that same morning. It was the consultant from Amaziteam as expected. It was time to talk openly and confidentially.

When Sophia put the receiver down half an hour later, she sat back and reflected on what had been a very interesting conversation.

That question about trust levels in the team had been hard to answer. Had she been too open? She did feel that there was a lack of trust between some members of the team. Stephen had asked them to be honest so she hoped she had done the right thing. She wondered if Christine would be as open.

***

Over in Stockholm, Anna was also reflecting on her call with Laura earlier that morning. She had to admit to herself that she hadn't been entirely honest with the consultant. As much as she wanted to trust Stephen as a leader, she was still cautious based on her previous experiences with unsupportive managers, which had made her question the value of honesty. Honesty may work on paper, but she wasn't sure that it worked in reality.

"How will it be when we're all together discussing these kinds of questions? It could get difficult, uncomfortable. How will everyone behave?" Anna felt a bit nervous. She didn't like conflict and worried there would be some. No, correction, she was pretty sure there would be some.

***

In London, the street noises fought loudly for Samuel's attention; an angry car horn, the squeaky breaks of a double-decker bus, a group of laughing teens, but he didn't hear any of it. He was folding a piece of paper, absent-mindedly, as he tried hard not to be affected by the prospect of the upcoming call.

"I don't want to talk to some consultant! How stupid!"

He wouldn't have admitted it to anyone, but he felt uncomfortable with the idea of talking to a stranger, or anyone for that matter, about his thoughts and feelings. It seemed like such a waste of time. He toyed with the idea of somehow blowing off the call with the consultant. He came to the conclusion that it would be easier to just do it, thereby flying under Stephen's radar. It would make no difference anyway, he reasoned. No-one could force him to do anything he didn't want to.

Stephen's Journal

*Good, now we have got the ball rolling. My initial conversation with the people at Amaziteam has made me feel good. In particular, it feels like I'm not alone in this, I've got some help and support, which to be honest, I need! I wouldn't want to say that to anyone, I hardly want to admit it to myself, but I **do** need help.*

I hope they will all be open and honest in their responses. If we are going to do all this, we have to do it properly, not just pay lip service. If there are problems, I need to know about them; we all need to know about them.

Chapter 12: Stephen talks to Helmut

"Ships in the harbor are safe, but that's not what ships are built for."

John A. Shedd

Stephen walked purposefully down the corridor to Helmut's office. It was on the 10th floor, the executive floor, which was still intact despite the cutbacks. Here the offices were large and imposing, with soft carpets and, Stephen noticed for the first time, no posters but genuine art on the walls. He thought it was funny how he had never noticed that before, despite having walked this corridor many times. His mind shot back to Samuel's comments about the art, or lack of it, in his office, and he had to admit that Samuel knew what he was talking about when it came to art.

Helmut's PA, a pretty brunette who had worked with Helmut since his BMW days, was on the phone. She smiled at Stephen and mouthed "please take a seat".

Stephen settled himself into the plush black leather settee in the waiting area outside Helmut's office. The office was glass-fronted, but the blinds were all down so he couldn't see Helmut. He assumed he was in there. He liked Helmut, in as much as he knew Helmut was a fair boss, and that was important to Stephen. He didn't necessarily feel comfortable with him though, and he couldn't quite work that out.

"I don't know why I feel that way. Maybe it's the fact that I just don't know him? I don't actually even know if he has a family! I know he's married, but I don't know if he has any kids. How strange not to know that about your boss! Why don't I know that? And why haven't I made an effort to find out if I think that's important? I know I've had a lot to think about since the merger, but this is one I've overlooked. Perhaps I should make an effort, work out how to get to know him a bit. Can I start today?"

Stephen shuffled his papers. If Alice had been there, she would have told him that this was something he always did when he was nervous or apprehensive.

"I wonder if my team feels comfortable with me. Have I given them enough of me to make them feel like they know me? I hadn't really considered that. I hope people find me approachable and friendly, as well as efficient and competent of course! I'm pretty sure people know that they can come and talk to me, that I will be fair and listen."

"OK Stephen, you can go on in now".

Stephen semi-hesitated in the doorway to the big corner office. He put his head around the door and Helmut waved him in.

He sat down opposite Helmut, in the same place he would always sit. It felt comfortable and uncomfortable at the same time.

His one-to-ones with Helmut were usually structured and time-efficient, with Helmut controlling the agenda. Today was the same, but Stephen also wanted to bring up the subject of his own leadership. He felt heartened by the customer results for Scandinavia they had just reviewed, which were trending positively. His mind was made up. He was going to take the bull by the horns and talk to Helmut about this, even though it was not something Helmut would normally spend much time on.

He had thought about how to bring up the subject, but had decided that there was only one way with Helmut; to just say it:

"I want to talk about my leadership."

Helmut raised his left eyebrow and said: "Yes?"

"I have had some feedback on my leadership lately that's made me aware that I could do more as a leader of my team." He looked at Helmut to gauge his reaction. Was this a good idea?

"So what's the feedback? What's your concern?"

"Umm.....I haven't been quick enough to get the team aligned and this has created some confusion, I'm afraid. I think the recent customer issue is a reflection of how important that alignment is. So I am taking firm action now. I'm running an alignment session with the team next week which I am confident will give us the results we want".

"Yes, I agree, you need to take charge and get it right".

Stephen nodded and got himself ready to ask Helmut for feedback, this had to be done. But before he'd had time to do so, Helmut volunteered:

"Not all your team members are with you, you know, and this is not OK, you're probably aware that Samuel came to talk to me..." Helmut waited for Stephen's acknowledgement. There was a moment of hesitation followed by relief as Stephen appreciated Helmut's straight talking. Stephen nodded as if in slow motion.

"It's affecting the trust in you, *your* team and *now* it's hitting the customers. You need to sort it out. I think you have what it takes and I think the rest of the team is with you, so go and do what you need to do to make that team successful. I want to see some results" he barked.

Stephen had been listening to Helmut when the realisation of Samuel's lie hit him. Samuel had gone to see Helmut, not the other way around as he had intimated. Anger shot through him and he had to force himself to focus his attention back on what his leader was saying.

"Yes, I'll get the results". He felt determined and his voice reflected that determination.

The one-to-one was wrapped up promptly as the PA entered the room, pointed to her watch and said efficiently:

"Your call is waiting".

Helmut lifted the receiver and was moving on swiftly to his next agenda item, seemingly not bothered by the conversation they'd just had. Stephen left the office and became conscious of the fact that Helmut would never provide him with the kind of support and easygoing relationship he would have liked from his leader. He would just have to settle for his trust and make sure he could go it alone.

Stephen's Journal

So now the Team Climate Study is complete. The consultant called the last couple of team members yesterday. I can't help but be a bit curious.

This team session will be different. It must, must work. I think it will, but I guess you never really know until you're there. Gerry trusts Laura though, she did wonders for his team, I'm sure she'll do the same for my team. And now Helmut has expectations as well. I can't afford to mess this up.

I will survive! I will be successful! I will make it work! And I will do it despite sneaky Samuel. He blatantly lied to me about his conversation with Helmut. What's he like? Well, I've decided I'm going to watch him very closely and I'm going to confront him as things happen going forward. If need be, I will do it in front of the team. He has undermined me enough.

Alice told me today that she thinks I'm being too tough on myself. She reminded me to journal the good things I'm doing as well, so here we go:

- *The customer satisfaction rates are up*
- *I had a good one-to-one with Anna on the phone today*
- *When I get to spend time with people I seem to connect with them and am able to motivate them. That's good, isn't it?*

It feels strange to write all this down. I don't want to appear arrogant or too confident. Although I doubt that would ever happen ☺.

OK, I'm officially tired, time for bed, signing off. Good night!

Chapter 13: It's all in the planning

"For I dipped into the future, far as the human eye could see, saw the vision of the world, and all the wonder that would be."

Alfred Lord Tennyson

Stephen was hurrying down Oxford Street, weaving in and out of the countless tourists, on his way to the restaurant. Laura from Amaziteam had suggested they meet at a restaurant close to Tottenham Court Road underground station. She had suggested that meeting away from the office would help him focus on the task at hand; the analysis of the team interviews and the planning of the upcoming Amaziteam session.

Stephen looked at his watch. The beautiful September day seemed to have brought everyone out into the street, which didn't help Stephen; he was already a few minutes late. He picked up the pace. He was eager to find out about the interviews. What had his team been saying?

"Ah, here we are," he thought. He pushed the door open and stepped in to the quiet restaurant. It was past the lunchtime rush, which he was pleased about. He spotted Laura across the room and made his way to the large table in the corner. He noticed, appreciatively, that it was away from the other

tables. That way, no-one would overhear their conversation; this needed to be a really open discussion.

Laura held out her hand: "Good to see you again, Stephen".

Stephen smiled: "And you, Laura"

After they had ordered their lunch, Laura said: "OK, should we get started?"

"Absolutely. I'm keen to hear what the team said."

"Yes, we'll get to that, but first let's talk about some of the practicalities regarding the session. As we discussed earlier, it needs to be held offsite, not in the office. We need people to shift their mindset from their day-to-day tasks and get into a different frame of mind. The environment can help that happen. It is of great importance to the outcome. How people feel will impact the level of success you achieve. Have you looked at any possible venues yet?"

"Yes, I've had some thoughts. I started looking at some of the usual options of conference venues, but due to the current cost restraints I was wondering if we could hold it at one of the other Black Sparrow offices, where most people haven't been before. It would still be like being away from the office. "

"Well, it won't be as good. We'll still have a good session but you won't get the impact you could have in the right setting.

As getting the results is important to you all, I would strongly recommend that we find an offsite location. It's not that I want you to spend money unnecessarily. Let me explain why this is so important."

Stephen smiled to himself as he remembered how the famous article had praised straight-talk. Laura sure was demonstrating that. He was curious about what she was going to say next.

Laura continued: "When people find themselves in an inspiring environment, they get a new outlook, they have new ideas, a different perspective, and they stop and reflect. Any kind of normal office setting hinders that. Last week I worked with a team at one of the country's most famous sport stadiums. When it came to creating the ground rules for the team, they had the creative idea to label those rules after the stadium. Now they can remember them in connection with the venue and what it felt like when they were there, making it easier to live by them and keep them alive. They also started looking at themselves in a different context, seeing the connection between how they work as a team and how a successful sports team needs to operate. The environment facilitated that. They relaxed and were able to be more open and honest with each other. The team formula is about making that honest and respectful interaction possible. We create that, with the help of the surroundings. If there is any way you can find the funding, it will make a difference."

Laura looked at Stephen, waiting for a comment.

"OK, I'll find the money. And if we're going down that route, I have a place in mind. As you were talking, I was reminded of River Castle, do you know it?"

"No, where is it?"

"It's in Oxford, it sits on the river. It's one of those cool old buildings with a lot of character in a dramatic setting. I've decided to hold the session in the UK this time. Most of us are located here anyway so that'll cut down on some of the expenses."

"Perfect," thought Laura. *"A true learning environment, what could be better? I won't point it out though; I'll let them find it out for themselves."*

"Sounds great, I think you should book it." Laura said. "Let's get into the planning of the session. We have two whole days and one evening. Will people be arriving the day before?"

"Yes, I think so, especially as some team members will be flying in".

"So the first time everyone will be together officially will be when we start on day 1 at 9.00am."

They were interrupted by the arrival of the waiter bringing their lunch, and abandoned their work conversation to eat.

After lunch, they went through and agreed the structure for the two days. Stephen talked about his observations of the team and the various members. He found it easy to talk to Laura about Samuel. It felt liberating to be able to talk so freely with someone, especially knowing that there would be a solution. He was also happy to have handed over the facilitation to someone else, so that he could participate and be a team member. He really wanted to observe Samuel in this setting too.

As the structure was agreed, Stephen asked eagerly: "Is it time for the Team Climate Study results?"

Laura shared a summary of the Team Climate Study with Stephen. The interview process had undoubtedly made the team think about how everything was working and Stephen became conscious of how valuable that alone was. The process of transformation had already started. She explained that the details would be shared with the whole team when they came together, and that the team would work through the findings and the solutions together. This was not solely the responsibility of Stephen so there was no reason for him to go through all the data himself. Stephen would have liked to know more, but decided to trust Laura and the process. He would just have to wait.

Stephen's Journal

Interesting meeting with Laura. I think we will have a good session. I'm a bit worried about not being in control of the outcome though. I don't quite understand how it will all work, but Laura assures me that it's supposed to be that way. I'm used to being in control, I'm the leader. What will it be like to have a facilitator? I like the idea but I'm not used to it. I must be patient, which is not always that easy! I can do it though. Although Alice might not agree, she thinks I'm very impatient. ☺

Chapter 14: The dreaming spires of Oxford

"You cannot open a book without learning something."

Confucius

The city of Oxford is dominated by its famous university. It was founded in 1096 and is the second oldest university in the world.

Scores of the city's buildings, including some of the famous colleges, are built from the distinctive Oxfordshire limestone, a creamy pale yellow colour. For decades this place of learning has attracted scholars, artists, writers and visitors. In contrast to the calm majesty of the buildings, the streets are filled with a variety of colourful bikes. They seem to buzz with activity as students and academics dash from place to place. It was, without a doubt, a truly unique place for the team session.

*

JR was the first to arrive. He was pleased to arrive early as it gave him the chance to take a walk around Oxford. As he walked down the High Street he felt very reflective.

"It's old, yet very young, this city of eternal youth and learning".
There was something in the air that JR couldn't quite put his
finger on. The old buildings, the winding streets all screamed
of history, yet the young people in the street gave the place a
sense of energy, hope, aspiration for a bright future. He had
never been to Oxford before and was wildly excited about all
that history. At the same time, he had to admit that he was a
little apprehensive about the two days ahead. He didn't know
what had happened after he had told Stephen about Samuel.
*"How are these next two days going to work, I wonder? I hope it'll
be a good use of all our time"* he thought as he watched a young
woman reading a book on the riverbank. At that exact
moment she looked up, saw him looking at her, and smiled
gently. JR grinned back, and felt inspired by that youthful
radiance. He continued his solitary walk with renewed
energy, map in hand.
"It will be good to see the others again, especially Sophia". He was
looking forward to the coming days.

*

Sophia pulled up outside the River Castle. She loved driving
and had offered to give Stephen, Christine and Samuel a ride
from the office. Samuel had said he would make his own way
and would arrive late that evening. The other two were happy
to accept and they had had a good opportunity for a catch-up
on the way there.

The River Castle Hotel, despite its size, was hidden away
behind the glass houses by the river. It was surprisingly quiet
considering it was right in the city centre.

"This looks like a nice place!" Sophia exclaimed.

Stephen and Christine both nodded enthusiastically. Christine actually looked more enthusiastic than Stephen had seen her in a long time. That bode well.

The limestone building had two turrets protruding proudly through the solid structure. The front lawn was shaded by a dramatic cedar tree lodged solidly next to the gatehouse at the entrance of the property.

It had been sunny and warm for days if not weeks now, but as they had entered Oxford, it started to cloud over. The heat was stifling, *"very unusual for late September"*, reflected Christine as she reached for her bag in the back of the car.

"See you all for drinks in half an hour" said Stephen. He bounded towards the big oak door, which was ajar.

As Stephen and Sophia entered the hotel, Christine gazed across the meadow leading down to the river. At the riverbank, she spotted two squabbling ducks. *"I wonder if that will be us. And I wonder how Laura will use the answers from her interviews. What did I say? I can't remember... I know I was very honest, I hope it won't come back to haunt me".*

*

Like many of her fellow Swedes, Anna had spent a lot of time in England, and this particular city was one of her favourites. She enjoyed the taxi ride as it offered her a chance to just sit back and do nothing. She admired the tree lined avenues leading into the city, with row upon row of imposing late Victorian houses. *"This is England at its best"*, she thought. A big smile suddenly spread across her face as she spotted the "dreaming spires" of Oxford. She was looking forward to spending time with the team, even more so in this inspiring and educational setting. She trusted Stephen and was convinced that the next two days would be good for the team. As her taxi came to a final halt, she alighted with confidence.

*

Samuel was an academic at heart. He had studied History of Art at Cambridge. As much as he admired Oxford for its academic standing, it wasn't Cambridge. In his eyes, it would always come second. Samuel hoped that the session would be an academic exercise about teamwork, where they could all understand the concepts and work with them. He didn't like to have to interact too much with the team. Moreover, he doubted the value of having some external consultant run the session; *"Surely Stephen could do this himself, if he was a real leader?"*

*

"Good morning"

Laura was already in the room, setting up. She looked up as Christine stepped in quietly. As Christine extended her hand, her eyes glanced around the room, surprised at the strange set-up. The chairs were in a semi-circle and there were no tables in the room. It immediately felt different, more personal, intimate even. This is not how they would normally sit in a team meeting. It seemed like the barriers had been taken away.

The room was an old library and the walls were lined floor to ceiling with beautiful leather bound books. It had a calm feeling to it and the thick walls meant it was very quiet. There were windows on one side of the room, overlooking the River Cherwell. The other side of the room displayed a huge Inglenook fireplace. Above it hung a portrait of a young man. No-one had yet had time to read the fine print to figure out who he was. Either side of the fireplace, Laura had intentionally placed two flipcharts. One was currently blank, waiting to be used, but the other one blasted out a simple message: WELCOME! ☺

A few minutes later, everyone had arrived and quiet conversations had started up. They were sitting balancing hot drinks on their knees; it felt a bit unusual. The atmosphere was relaxed and light-hearted following the informal dinner the night before. Samuel hadn't made it in time to join the others for dinner, and was subsequently keeping a low profile.

"Where will you put your laptop, Samuel?" asked Anna cheekily in an attempt to draw Samuel into the conversation.

Samuel gave a dismissive shrug, and mumbled into his coffee.

At this point Stephen decided to start the session by welcoming his team to River Castle. As advised by Laura, he had thought extensively about his welcoming comments. He cleared his voice.

"I'm glad you're all here. The next two days are important for all of us. We are the leaders for all our people and if we are to be as successful as we can be, we need to work very effectively together. We have already identified that we are not, currently, a high-performing team. So we are here to change that. I am going to do everything in my power to make this happen and I expect the same from you. I want you to be fully engaged and participating 100% throughout."

He forced eye contact with Samuel, who stayed completely still.

"It's not just about what we do; it's about how we do it. It's so easy to focus on tasks and to-do-lists and get busy with that, which is of course important, but it's equally important to think about how we behave with each other and our teams. We need to consider our impact on the world around us. With the right behaviours, we will build trustful relationships, encourage teamwork, make people feel good about coming to work and contribute more to the bottom line. These are challenging times, the financial climate is tough, our competitors are good and we have to be better. The only thing that can differentiate us from our competitors is HOW we do things, which is particularly important for us to deliver our service experience. This is a great investment of both time and money, it is aimed at our development and your proactive participation is of paramount importance to the return on that investment."

He had their attention even though his opening comments seemed more corporate than personal.

"I'm going to hand over to Laura who will facilitate this process for us. I will be a proactive participant just like you, because I'm also a member of this team, not just its leader. I'll let Laura introduce herself. Over to you" he gestured at Laura.

"Good morning all and welcome, I'm Laura from Amaziteam. I'm delighted to meet you all face to face. It's also great to have had the opportunity to talk to you during the climate study calls and gain an understanding of your team. Let me share a bit of my background. I've been with Amaziteam for 10 years. We are a straight-talking global consultancy that works with organisations that realise that they can do more. Organisations are led by people, so we work with the people to make them drivers of success. How leaders act and behave impacts their teams. How teams act and behave impacts other teams and the customers. All of this creates a culture of either success or mediocrity, or in really bad cases, failure. So in challenging times in particular, organisations who invest in the human interactions at work are more successful. Before I joined Amaziteam, I held various leadership positions in the financial industry, so I know what it's like to be a leader and a team member, just like you. On a personal note I live close to

Reading in the UK. I am married and have a 12 year-old daughter. I am on a constant learning journey and I find that I learn from all the teams I work with and all the individuals I meet. It's also incredible how much you can learn from a 12 year-old" she flashed them a smile. "I look forward to learning with you over the next couple of days. I am here to help *you* be more successful. How do you feel about that?"

"Sounds good" chirped JR. The others nodded carefully.

Chapter 15: The transformation – Opening up

"Telling the truth is easier than hiding it, and so much easier to remember."

"To start off I would like you to share something about yourself. It can be whatever you like. Your only constraint is that I would like you to share something that your colleagues don't know about you."

Laura led the introductions, encouraging the six team members to share a part of themselves with the rest of the team. It was an important step. This wasn't just about business; they had to bring their whole person to the session, not just their work persona. This was the first part of the formula, helping them to find their way.

With his characteristic smile, JR surprised his colleagues with the revelation that he had started a band while in high school. Furthermore, as he delighted in telling them, he was still playing in it. Samuel opened up by sharing his dedication for art; he was clearly very knowledgeable on the subject. He got carried away with his descriptions and reluctantly reined himself in after some gentle prompting from Laura. The team had never heard him talk so passionately about anything. They found out about Anna's passion for travelling, especially to cities. Christine revealed that she spends some of her spare time with a charity, reading for blind people. Stephen shared his love for fast cars and, receiving appreciative glances and some laughs, he revealed that his first car was a 1961 Jaguar E type. Sophia was a regional tennis champion at the age of 15 and still actively plays tennis several times a week; naturally this was met by JR challenging her to game.

Once the personal introductions were completed, Laura thanked them and went straight into action. Despite the sharing there was still some tension in the air so Laura's main focus was to get started and get the team into the flow of the session quickly.

"Let's agree how our time together will work. What ground rules do we want to set for ourselves? What should we do or not do while we are here in this room?" She moved her arm in a sweeping motion from side to side; it was obvious she meant the space in the room.

Laura let her words sink in. There were a few quiet moments where each person was thinking about what she had said. *"What do we really want?"* This was harder to articulate than they could have imagined.

After a few minutes the first contribution was made hesitantly. It was Stephen's.

"I think we should really *be* here, and be committed, so no phones, no Blackberries, no interruptions basically."

"This is a big investment in time and money, and we mustn't waste it," he thought to himself.

His suggestion was met with some scepticism.

"But my team may need to get hold of me!" exclaimed JR.

"You can deal with that in the breaks. Manage your team's expectations; let them know that you will not be able to return their calls immediately."

"Yes, true, I guess" said JR. He looked at his colleagues. He knew he would not have been alone in his initial reaction.

Another idea was offered. This time it was Anna.

"I think we need to be honest, otherwise what's the point?"

"Sure" said JR.

"Well, if I'm going to be honest, I want this to be confidential. Can we do the Vegas rules? What is said in the room, stays in the room?" Sophia managed to combine seriousness with an injection of humour, she winked at Anna.

"Sounds reasonable"

"How about being constructive, so we don't feel like we're being personally attacked?"

Christine twisted her body sideways, awkwardly. "Respect is important to me" she continued.

"Shouldn't we respect each others' time by being back on time after breaks?" Sophia added.

"Yeah, good one"

"Stephen mentioned active participation so let's add that to the list" Christine said.

Laura was furiously scribing the suggestions on a flipchart.

"Let's make sure we come up with some tangible actions to take away" said Samuel.

"Are we allowed to have fun?" smiled Anna.

"Oh, I should hope so" Stephen retorted.

As no more ideas were forthcoming, Laura probed: "When you said honest, tell me more about what you were thinking?" She looked at Anna.

"So often we just say that we're honest when all we're really doing is saying what we think people want to hear, or skirting around the subject. If we are really open, we share our concerns, we voice our opinions. So maybe we should just be a bit more passionate and say it as it is." She hesitated "At the same time as being respectful of course. I think we have to assume positive intent. Can we add that?" She pointed at the pen in Laura's hand.

"Great" Laura said "I think that makes it very clear. Do you all agree?"

She got their agreement. Laura tore off the page from the flipchart that she had been writing on and moved with it over to the other side of the room.

"OK, good, I'll put these on the wall for you and you can hold each other accountable to them."

"Now I'd like you to seriously think about what you intend to get out of these days. What are your expectations? What will you make happen? What would be a good outcome for you from this session? You are responsible for the value you get out of this session, so you need to be proactive about choosing your outcome".

Laura's words created a profound insight for Sophia. "*It's so simple, but so true. I hadn't really thought about it in those terms before, that I need to know my outcome in order to get to it. My outcome is my responsibility so therefore our outcome is our responsibility. That makes a lot of sense. I wish I had thought more about what I want out of this session before today, to have been better prepared. Never mind, I'll do it now."*

"I want us to become a team" said Sophia.

"I want to get to know people better" said Anna.

"I want to learn more about myself and the team" said JR.

"I want to learn how we can work better together" said Stephen.

Similar thoughts were re-iterated in different ways by different people, creating four key themes:

- Get to know each other
- Learn something new
- Create a strong team
- Work better together

Laura continued, pushing them further, "I'd also like you to share how you feel, right here, right now".

Over the next few minutes they individually wrote down their feelings on post-it notes and attached them to a flipchart. These read:

- Curious
- Interested
- Optimistic
- Confident
- Anxious
- Cautious
- Excited
- Thoughtful
- Undecided

After having shared their individual reflections and expectations, Laura asked: "How did you find that exercise?"

There was a pause before Stephen said: "Actually, it was harder to share how I feel than I thought it would be. Also, everyone just shared such a range of feelings, from cautious all the way to excited. Is that normal in teams?" He looked enquiringly at Laura.

"Yes, perfectly normal. You're a team coming together and you're all coming from different places. It's about you learning to express how you feel. Indeed, learning to feel safe conveying your feelings in a work setting. It takes trust; it's all about the level of trust in the team. In high-performing teams they all share very openly how they feel at any given time, not just what they think. If you're not used to doing it, of course it will take some practice. You've made a good start."

Stephen observed how vulnerable he had felt when he had shared with the team that he was anxious about the next steps; that he felt a bit out of control going into a process that he was not familiar with, not knowing quite how it would work. But his ambition was to encourage the others to open up and be honest, and in order for that to happen, he knew he had to lead the way, to set an example.

"So how much do you share with each other about how you feel?" Laura asked bluntly.

"Not much, I don't think. There hasn't really been an opportunity, or even a reason to do it." Emboldened by Stephen's frankness, Christine continued: "Recently I've been having some personal issues. I think that if I had been open about how I felt, I would have been afraid to have my feelings overflow; like that time when we went quad biking and I started crying."

Samuel shifted uncomfortably in his seat and Stephen lowered his eyes in memory of how difficult he had found that situation, how difficult he found the sudden expression of feelings.

"Thanks for sharing" Laura waited a moment but as no more comments were coming forward, she decided to leave it there for now.

The silence was interrupted by the distinctive sounds of the Christ Church bells. The harmonious tones of the twelve bells flowed across the meadow and filled the room, indicating change.

"It's time for a break. Coffees and teas are outside, let's come back again in 15 minutes."

During the break, Anna noticed that she felt closer to her colleagues than she had done before. It was as if a bit of the armour had come down. *"Interesting feeling"*, she thought.

Chapter 16: The Transformation – Diving Deeper

"A boat doesn't go forward if each one is rowing their own way."

Swahili proverb

"As you are all aware, as part of the preparation for this session, I interviewed each of you in order to understand what it's like to work in this team. Now it's time to look at the results, together. You're going to get the chance to analyse these responses, anonymously, and decide what to do. So, let me tell you more about how this process is going to work..."

Laura explained that they would divide into two groups. Each group was to review and discuss one half of the results from the Team Climate Study, with the purpose of identifying key themes rather than individual comments. As Laura pointed out, they would have to trust the other group to review and report back honestly on behalf of the whole team.

As agreed with Stephen beforehand, Laura indicated that Stephen, Samuel and Sophia would form one group, and JR, Christine and Anna would make up the other. Quietly, they moved into the two designated groups and sat down. Laura then handed each of them a report. They had 20 minutes to read it, individually, before starting the discussion.

The report may as well have been a hot potato, the way the team members tentatively received it. A single question was on everyone's mind: *"What will we find out?"*

Christine was wondering if everyone had been as honest as she had. Would her answers really stand out and identify her? She felt her breath quicken and her eyes darted around the room, looking for reassurance. There was none to be had. Everyone, apart from Samuel, was already busy reading. The room had gone quiet as heads bent in concentration.

Samuel sighed and slumped in his chair, demonstratively showing his reluctance.

"Remind me again, what am I supposed to be doing? Do I have to read it all?" Samuel queried, seemingly not having listened to the instructions.

Laura smiled and repeated her instructions, this time more slowly and deliberately, indicating that Samuel's group only needed to read the first half of the report.

Samuel didn't respond, but opened the report slowly and seemed to be starting to read.

The room was still. The silence only interrupted by the occasional rustles of turning pages and the ticking clock on the mantelpiece. It was getting warm; Laura opened a window. The wooden frame of the window creaked and settled, and now the sound of the gardener trimming the old box hedge filtered through.

A sharp intake of breath came from Sophia's direction. Stephen quickly looked over: "What is it?"

"Oh, I'm just surprised at some of the comments about how we use our time in meetings. There are some extremely differing views here. It's fascinating."

Stephen had made the same reflection. It was becoming apparent that this process would bring some of the issues out onto the table more effectively than he could ever have done himself. He adjusted his weight on the chair, feeling uncomfortable. Not physically uncomfortable, but emotionally uncomfortable, and not necessarily in a negative way. His discomfort was intermingled with hope that this would genuinely make a difference. Laura had warned him that he might, at times, feel uncomfortable. In their meeting she had reminded him that he needed to be courageous and willing to disclose more than he would normally do; "showing strength by being vulnerable" she had called it. He took a sip of his coffee, which had gone unforgivably cold, and shuddered. It tasted sour. He abruptly put the mug down and pushed it away.

When just over 20 minutes had passed, Laura cleared her throat and invited them to continue the journey: "It looks like you've all finished reading so I'd like you to huddle up in your smaller groups and have your discussions. What did you find? And what are you going to do about it? Are you all clear on what to do?" Laura's eyes wandered over the group, noting nods and acknowledgments all around.

Samuel, Stephen and Sophia moved closer together. Stephen waved the report and said: "There's an awful lot in here, isn't there?"

"Yes, well, what if we start with my observation about the varying views on how we spend our time together? Some people feel there is no value in our meetings and that it's more time consuming than anything else." Sophia glanced at Samuel and continued without breaking her pace, "Other people, however, think that it's been useful to share and get to know each other better. So maybe we actually just need to agree how those meetings and any of our interactions, like emails, calls, conference calls, need to work. What *should* we be doing with our time together?"

"To be honest, I don't think we need to spend that much time together." Samuel said abruptly. "Once a month is plenty, and one hour is probably enough, a quick update from everyone and then any corporate information from Stephen".

"Fair enough that you have your views, but as you can see from the report there are other people that see it differently, and that needs to be taken into account. We all have a responsibility for the whole team, not just ourselves." This was turning into a real eye opener. Stephen was just thinking how selfish Samuel was; it was becoming clearer by the minute that he didn't want to be a part of the team. And it wasn't just Stephen's imagination, Samuel was pretty much saying so. *"If someone doesn't want to be a team member then can the team trust him?"* Stephen scratched his head and reflected silently on what to do next. *"Should I confront Samuel about it or just wait it out?"* Before he'd had time to do anything, Sophia continued her animated observations:

"Another thing I picked up was the trust thing. There are a lot of comments in this report that we are not open, really open, with each other. We don't share what's going on in our personal lives or at work. Is that trust? Could it be that we don't know each other?" Sophia paused, jumped up and grabbed a marker pen by the flipchart. She was clearly enjoying the process and throwing herself into it one hundred percent. Without hesitation she started writing:

- Time and purpose of our meetings
- Trust. Getting to know each other?

"Do you agree? Is that it?"

She looked at Stephen, who added: "Yes, there's plenty in here about how we need to get a better grip on our meetings and how we spend our time together to make it useful to everybody, so I think we have to address that. Everyone needs to agree and commit to whatever we decide. Our agreement to answer emails within 24 hours is mentioned in the report; there are several references to how that didn't fully work. Samuel, I know in this case that these comments were about you, and I don't want to harp on about old stuff, but from now on what the team agrees must be upheld by all.

Are you prepared to do that? I don't think we can move on unless you are." Stephen surprised not only Samuel and Sophia, but also himself, by his directness.   He was strengthened by the consistent feedback from the rest of the team, clearly described through the interviews. It gave him the permission to confront Samuel, knowing that his team was behind him, these weren't just his views.

In fact, their views, outlined in the team climate survey, had somehow been transformed from what could be a sensitive thing into an objective observation. In black and white, the team members' views had become tangible, actionable opportunities that were OK to explore and discuss.

"Are you prepared to stick to team agreements?" Stephen looked Samuel in the eye with intensity.

Samuel avoided his direct eye contact, studying the face in the portrait above the fireplace instead.

The tension mounted while Stephen waited for a response. Finally, he got it.

"Yes, I can see from this report that this is important to people, so assuming that it's something I can agree with, then sure, I'll do it". Samuel picked his words carefully, without looking up.

"Good" Stephen said. Inwardly he thought: *"I must come back to that. I'm not sure he will do it unless I stay on his case"*. He continued:

"There is a big theme in here about openness, or the lack of it, which is probably due the lack of trust. We don't really share how we truly feel about situations at work. I believe it's either due to a fear of what others might think or say about us, or what they might do with that information. We don't seem to have the time to talk either. Could we make time for that in our meetings?"

Sophia added 'Openness' as a bullet point to the list.

Across the room, the other group was deep in conversation. They were animated and it was clear that they were all engaged in the task.

Christine's fear had been eradicated, as everyone had indeed been open and the report showed a number of honest comments. She was relieved and now eager to put her focus on the team.

JR had been put in charge of scribing. He was pacing by his flipchart with the report open showing several bright highlights. He spotted that Sophia was in charge at the other flipchart. He caught her eye and exchanged a smile with her for a brief moment, before firmly placing his focus back on his small group.

"There's some great stuff in here, guys! It's showing all of the issues that I have experienced. I'm excited about getting this fixed, which we should be able to do, given that we seem to have some similar views. There are some strong, clear themes, and together we can fix this! Right?" He grinned at Christine and Anna, pretty much expecting their agreement.

Anna couldn't help but smile back. JR had that effect on people; his enthusiasm was infectious when he got engaged in a subject.

"So what are the themes?"

Christine cleared her throat.

"We clearly have a problem with silo working. For example, that MIS palaver that cost us our customer, was due to our silos. I think it's fair to say that, currently, we just do not work together. We don't seem to share a common goal, or direction, or purpose, or whatever. We're all just so busy doing our own work. We obviously didn't communicate very well, did we?"

Both JR and Anna nodded vigorously, and JR wrote in bold capitals.

- WORKING IN SILOS
- COMMUNICATION (OR A LACK OF)

"You're both right. We just don't talk to each other; we don't tell each other what we're doing. I don't know what you're working on at the moment for example, JR. I don't know what's important to you, or what your priorities are. Maybe if I did, I could share things with you regarding what I have done. We could help and support each other much more, that's for sure. What if one of us is currently doing something brilliant but not letting the others know? Ultimately the customer loses out as they don't get the benefit of *all* our knowledge." Anna waited for a reaction from the others.

"That's easy for us to do something about. Maybe we should have '*sharing*' as an agenda item for our meetings? We don't do that now." JR said.

JR was animated and energised by the discussion and the searing bright insights they were having together. He was also surprised that it was going so well, that they seemed to be progressing so easily.

"I also spotted how we avoid conflict and if there is tension we ignore it, or we expect Stephen to deal with it. Don't we all have to take responsibility for that? Can we add 'Conflict Avoidance' to the list?" asked JR while already writing it on the flipchart.

Christine smiled at his obvious expectation that they would agree with him, which of course they did.

"Yes, unresolved conflict is a killer, but I have to admit that I find that difficult. Why didn't we go straight to Stephen with our concerns about the 24-hour email commitment that wasn't kept? Why did we just talk to a few people, behind each other's backs? I know you did it too." Christine looked knowingly at her colleagues.

"That's another theme, isn't it?" exclaimed JR, jumping up again. "Let's add 'Keeping Team Commitments' to the list".

"Yes, because if we don't do that, then what happens to trust? If we can't trust each other then we'll just keep working independently."

JR wrote 'TRUST' on the flipchart and underlined it.

They continued working intensively and time seemed to just disappear. When Laura did a time check with the two teams, they both indicated that they needed more time. She smiled and nodded, holding up both hands, fingers spread out, indicating they could have another 10 minutes. This certainly wasn't the first team she had met who had thrown themselves in fully once the flood gates were open.

She reminded them that they needed to be focusing on solutions now. From Laura's experience, teams always needed more time once the talking had started to flow, yet they needed to be prompted to drive towards the solutions and actions too.

Fifteen minutes later, Laura invited the two groups to come back as one.

The chairs shuffled softly over the thick Oriental rug as they all moved back into a semicircle. Compared to just a few hours earlier, this set-up felt much more comfortable now.

"Just before we go to lunch, tell me what it was like to go through that? Not the actual results, just what you experienced here". Laura made eye contact with each of them in turn.

"It was very interesting to see everyone's views" JR started.

"Tell me more about that" prompted Laura.

"The thing that struck me was that there were such opposed views at times. For example, someone had said that decisions are made by the whole team, whereas someone else said that all decisions are made by Stephen, or Helmut."

"And what does that tell you? What do you need to do with that as a team?"

"Well, what can we do? Different views are different views. I don't think we need to do anything with that. We're all entitled to our own view" Samuel sounded defensive.

Christine sighed, a long, loud sigh, not to be misunderstood. She looked at the ceiling, searching for words.

She didn't look at Samuel as she commented: "WE ARE HERE to work together as a team, so we should be looking for how we can somehow align our views at least, and share them. If there are such different views about how decisions work, we must explore what we see and hear that makes our experiences so different. And then we need to work out how to make decisions in the future. That is why we are here" she reiterated.

Most of her colleagues nodded, acknowledging her frustration. Samuel on the other hand had directed his attention to his watch; he deliberately brought his hand up to check the time.

"Well I found that going through that experience got us talking in a new way. All the issues were out in the open, in a safe way, so we could kind of talk about them without assigning blame. I felt like a consultant who could look at our team with fresh eyes, in a non-defensive way" Sophia contributed, ignoring the slight tense feeling created by Samuel's dissociation from the team.

"What about you, Anna?"

Anna was still thinking about wanting to raise her profile and getting people to listen to her, so she took a deep breath and summarised her thoughts:

"Up until now we haven't given ourselves time to talk about this. We're just busy, busy, busy, running around as if being busy makes us successful, well it doesn't. It's fundamental for us to have these discussions in order to be successful. The power for me was in the open discussions we've just had, in our sub-groups. I think we need to have them in this whole group too. For the first time, I feel we are more of a team. We are finally coming together on the same side with a common agenda. And if we're all on the same side, then there's nothing we can't do. Imagine the power of us all being on the same side; we're all clever people, imagine what we can achieve together. If we are all together, behind something, we would be completely unstoppable. We would multiply our learning, our output, our results. Doing so demands complete trust and willingness to let go of any territorial thinking or defensiveness. Then anything is possible. That's what I think we can get from this."

Anna's voice strengthened through her monologue and her eyes shone with passion. She didn't notice that the others had been leaning in to listen to her, their eyes widened, almost with a look of surprise. They were seeing Anna in a new light. In an unassuming way she was demanding their attention, and she got it.

Laura had been encouraging Anna through the address, subtly nodding as a sign of recognition. "Great observation, Anna. Let's leave it there for now. After lunch we'll come back and talk about your findings, as one team. We will take 58 minutes for lunch" Laura wrapped up the morning with a grin, and ushered an upbeat team out the door.

Chapter 17: Laughing at Lunch

"If you are too busy to laugh, you are too busy."

Proverb

Lunch was set up in the restaurant in the conservatory, where the lawn outside ran all the way down to the riverbank. The imposing main building of St Hilda's College stood proudly in the distance on the other side of the water.

The black and white tiled floor gave the restaurant an efficient flair. The grand arches of the conservatory windows meant the room was bright and airy. It was altogether a pleasant space, with a relaxed atmosphere.

Two other groups were seated for lunch as Stephen and his team were shown to the Black Sparrow table. As they took their seats, the waitress, with a welcoming smile, introduced the buffet table at the back of the room. When they were finally seated with their plates filled, Laura said: "Before you start…"

JR already had his fork in midair and froze. He thought that Laura was about to say grace: "*Maybe this is one of those Oxford traditions?*"

"... your lunch" continued Laura "I'd like to set another ground rule. Over lunch, please don't talk about work. You can discuss any subject, just not work, OK? Bon appétit!"

Laura observed how JR and Sophia started talking straight away, their heads bent towards each other, smiling and joking.

Samuel sat in silence and Laura was starting to see the impact he was having on the team. Anna struck up a conversation, asking him about his interest in art, which he had mentioned in the library that morning. Samuel started a long lecture on cubism and Picasso's inimitable impact on it. Anna soon realised that Samuel wasn't going to ask anything about her, so she quietly settled down to listen.

"How are things with you now?" Stephen turned to Christine, leaving his question open, waiting to see how she would respond.

"I'm OK." Christine kept her distance by talking generally about how she was doing, avoiding the subject of her divorce. She knew she should probably start talking to people about it, especially her boss, but she just wasn't ready. "*Maybe I will be ready when we finish this session*", she thought.

An outburst of laughter from Sophia halted their conversations.

"What's so funny?" Anna welcomed the interruption. She looked enquiringly at Sophia, "Please share".

Sophia chuckled, "JR is so hilarious! He just makes me laugh. Do tell the others, JR!"

"Oh, it was just one of those language mix-ups between American and British English, a story of my missing pants. Needless to say, the British hotel was not too eager to go looking for my pants when my assistant called to say I had left them behind in the room. I'll leave it there" he said with a huge JR smile.

They were all howling with laughter and the lunch continued with the same light-hearted frivolity.

Laura leaned back and reflected on how the team was showing signs of opening up. Things were progressing as expected for this kind of session. It was forcing them to start to reflect on how they were working together, as well as just having some fun together and getting to know each other, something that was obviously starting to build trust. "*OK, let's get them back into the library and get straight-talking*".

Chapter 18: The Transformation – Deeper and Deeper

"Overcoming barriers to performance is how groups become teams."

Jon Katzenbach & Douglas Smith

"So what did you discover this morning?" queried Laura, having welcomed the group back to the library. "Which team would like to go first? This is an opportunity to let the other group know the contents of your half of the report, as they haven't read it yet. It would also be good to share the in-depth conversations you had in your group, and any particularly interesting points that need further discussion in the big group."

The next hour was spent deep in conversation; the team shared their findings, debated differences of opinion and tried to come up with a common view of the team's situation. Laura prompted them and moved the process forward, allowing them to struggle with some of the more difficult challenges, giving them time and space as a team to work through it. There was a different feeling in the room now. People were getting more comfortable, opening up more, not being as guarded, and starting to trust the process in earnest. At the end of it, a compiled list of findings was created on the flipchart. It read:

WHAT we do

- Our purpose
- Do we need to be a team?
- Our roles and responsibilities
- Our work processes

HOW we do it

- Trust
  - Not being open
  - Don't know each other
  - Not sharing information
  - Not keeping team commitments
- Time together not spent in productive way
- Communication
  - Working in silos
  - Not sharing information and best practices
  - Not sharing concerns
  - Avoiding conflict
- Poor decision making

Good individuals

Excellent knowledge of business

We have potential as a team

This is easy to fix

Enjoy each others' company ☺

"Good, how do you feel about your list? Is there anything missing?" Laura asked.

"We've covered so much from this report, I don't really see that there is anything else" said JR. "What else are you looking for, Laura?" he quizzed her. He glanced at Stephen who had struck a good balance between listening and talking throughout the day. Stephen had learnt how brilliant it was to have Laura there; it allowed him to sit back and listen to the team, as well as being a member of the team. As a result, he was beginning to see the team members take ownership of the team. He'd been trying to achieve this for months, but up until now had not seen any results. At last, it was all happening in front of him.

"Well" said Laura "for me there is something missing here. I want you to consider your impact, and I mean your impact as a team, on the people around you, your stakeholders, the people that work for you, Helmut, customers and other partners that you interact with in the business. How do they perceive you? If I went to interview them about you, what would they say?"

"Oh, that's a very interesting point. I hadn't thought about that. Umm, I guess they would say that we don't really look like a team. They probably couldn't answer it as we aren't really a team." Sophia looked concerned with a furrowed brow.

Samuel tutted, raising his eyes to the ceiling in disdain: "Do you REALLY think that we have time in this business to go around worrying about what others think of us?" It was clearly a rhetorical question.

"Oh, come on Samuel, you can't say that *we* don't have a view on other teams, such as the Marketing team. We all think they don't talk to each other and neither do they seem to know what the others are working on. Now that I think about it, that actually damages their reputation. So guess what, if we don't consider this then our reputation may stop us from achieving our goals, and to be honest, may negatively impact my career, and yours!" Christine blurted out, cheeks flushed with annoyance. Samuel was getting on her frazzled nerves and she made no attempt to hide it.

Stephen decided to jump in: "I know what Helmut thinks of us. He thinks we don't work together as a team; he blames us for losing that customer, and I mean all of us, not just me. As a result, he doesn't trust us at the moment, so he won't give us greater responsibility. More responsibility could have helped us move towards our ambition, in the direction of proactive customer relationship management. So perception is crucial to our success, let's not kid ourselves that it's not."

"So, are you all in agreement with that?" said Laura, looking at Samuel. They all nodded except for Samuel who gave a slight shrug, which seemed to mean *"OK, if I have to"*.

As a result, Laura added 'Perception and Impact' to the 'HOW we do it' list.

The room was getting warm again. The rays of the afternoon sun highlighted the dust particles in the room, dancing in midair. Sophia gazed with envy at what looked like a group of students having a picnic by the river. They were laughing and pointing at someone punting down the Cherwell, and she wanted to transport herself into the sunshine, where they were. But as this was not possible, she settled for opening a window and took a deep breath, inhaling the warm, pleasant air.

"OK, let's look at the list again. What else do you think we need to do about all this now? Laura asked.

The team members thought they had done what they were supposed to do, so they hesitated, not quite knowing what was expected of them.

Stephen gave Laura an inquisitive look, indicating that he wasn't sure either.

"What you have here is a good and concise description of current issues and what the team needs." She paused for effect and then continued, "But HOW are you going to do this? For example, what are you going to do to BE OPEN to build TRUST? How will that happen? What do you need to say and do, when, and to whom?"

"Oh, I see what you mean. We need to be more specific. Well, I imagine we would need to ask for help, admit when we are challenged by a situation. And even just tell each other what we are doing. Maybe there should be a slot for that in our team meetings".

"Yes, I agree, Anna, they're good solutions. Let's take those as an action" said Stephen.

"So how are you going to hold each other accountable?" Laura said and pointed at the bullet point of 'not keeping team commitments', "What if someone goes against what you have agreed?"

All eyes were instantly on Samuel.

"Look, I really want to say this. And this feels like the right time. I want to tell you how upset I was when you so blatantly disregarded our 24-hour email agreement, Samuel" Sophia stared at Samuel, unblinking.

"We had all agreed, including you, but there you were, just not doing it, and not even apologising for it. It was as if you put yourself above the rules; that they simply didn't apply to you. Yet you agreed to make that rule. Before that, I sort of respected you, but since then I don't trust you, and I don't trust that you won't do it again. Furthermore, I question your motive, why would you behave like that with your own team members?"

Laura intervened "So, how did that make you feel, Sophia?"

"Angry, disappointed, frustrated" she said very quickly, as if she had been waiting to blurt out her feelings.

Everyone was motionless through the exchange. The rug was being intensely scrutinised as no-one looked directly at anyone else.

"So Samuel, how do you feel about this?" Laura asked.

"I don't think anyone else here feels like you do, Sophia" he gestured around the room.

"Well actually, she's not alone" JR said. "I agree with every word. It made me feel like you have your own hidden agenda. It made me feel disappointed and it's made me avoid you as much as I can. I certainly wouldn't go out of my way to help you, which is crazy to say about a team member. It shouldn't be like that."

Anna and Christine nodded in unison. Stephen shifted nervously in his chair.

Laura left a gap of silence to allow that tough statement to sink in with everybody. "*This is good*", she thought, "*this is a break-through*".

Samuel looked deep in thought, still inspecting the Oriental rug. He opened his mouth, hesitated and closed it again as if he was searching for the right words. "*What have I done? Not*

sure how to get out of this. I didn't realise this was such a big deal.
Why are these people taking it so personally? I just thought it was a
stupid rule, I didn't think it would make any difference. I've always
worked on my own, and now it feels like I'm being forced to work
with them. What am I going to say now?"

After a long silence, Samuel opened his mouth.

"I had no idea that this was such a big deal for you all. I
didn't realise the impact I was having and I didn't think you
guys were paying that much attention to what I was doing, to
be honest. Clearly, I will have to think about this in the future.
It was not my intention to upset you." Samuel stopped
abruptly.

"OK, so what about any agreements we make here? Will you
stick to them?" JR continued.

"Yes, I will." It was obvious that Samuel wanted to cut the
conversation short. He felt more and more uncomfortable and
clearly wanted to leave the room.

"Do you know what, Samuel, it wasn't just about you in that
example. If we're being honest here, and it now feels like we
are, it was also about us letting you get away with it.
Especially you, Stephen" Emboldened by the previous
exchange, Anna spoke up.

"We were, or maybe I should just speak for myself, *I* was
disappointed in you. I was disappointed that you let Samuel

do as he wished. I expected you to hold Samuel accountable. I thought it was your job as our leader. I *do* think you are good leader, so I was even more surprised, and felt even more let down." Anna paused.

Samuel squirmed.

Stephen was relieved this had been raised now and that it was Anna who did it. He had expected this. Laura had told him to be brave and demonstrate vulnerability, as this would encourage the other team members to let their guard down too.

"You are right; I didn't handle that very well. I thought the situation would just sort itself out. I guess I thought you would eventually get in line, Samuel, and do as we had agreed."

JR interrupted: "But it wasn't just the one time, now was it, Samuel? You've continued to not respond to team emails when everyone else has. It's just not fair and it's not good for the team."

JR straightened his back unconsciously, as if he was trying to make himself as imposing to Samuel as possible.

Seemingly undaunted by JR's attack, Samuel muttered: "OK, I've said I'm going to do it. Can we just leave it now?" He looked down, his mind racing: "*I don't want to be here. I hate doing this. How can I get out of this? What time is it? How much longer are we doing this?"*

Stephen was given another opportunity to demonstrate his leadership there and then.

"So why didn't you, Samuel? Why didn't you stick to that very simple agreement?"

"As I've just said, I didn't think it was a big deal. OK, I now understand it is" Samuel retorted, rolling his eyes. He tried to cut the conversation short once again.

Reading the dynamics of the room, Laura stood up to let the team know she was taking control of the focus of the conversation. They all looked at her, relieved, as they didn't know what to do.

"Christine, you've been a little quiet" Laura said softly. "Would you like to share your thoughts?"

"Yes, I would" Christine replied after a short pause. "I think we are all senior enough to have been able to challenge Samuel, it wasn't just Stephen's job. Personally I had too much going on in my life at the time to gather up the energy to fight this battle too."

Laura nodded.

Stephen spoke up again. "I am sorry that I let you all down on this, and I mean all of you. I also let Samuel down by not being clear about what's acceptable and not. This should have been clear enough as it was, but since it didn't work, I should have followed up on it."

Samuel was taken aback, causing him to jolt back deeper into his chair.

"I won't do it again. I will hold you all accountable going forward and I expect you to do the same, to me and to each other. This is an excellent example of what happens if we don't. So while we're on the subject of honest feedback, do you have any other feedback for me?" Stephen looked purposefully around the room at his team.

Laura held up her hand: "Before anyone answers, and that is a brilliant question, Stephen, we will be giving each other some feedback tomorrow. So I want you to reflect overnight on any feedback you want to give to each other. I'll take you through a simple process for that tomorrow before we get started. So sorry, Stephen, you're just going to have to wait until then" Laura grinned at him.

Stephen was a bit annoyed that Laura had stopped him, but he had complete faith in her and the process so he decided to leave it. He sensed that the group was not too eager about the announced feedback session though. This had been challenging enough for one day.

"What you've just done is clarify what it takes to hold each other accountable. You have been open, you have challenged both Samuel and Stephen on the occasions when they did not take responsibility for agreements or assumed agreements. So what does it feel like now that is all out in the open?" Laura let the question linger.

A brief silence was broken by a humming sound from Anna, followed by Sophia's exclamation:

"It feels better now that we've said it. I hope it makes a difference, and I think it will. We've never spoken this openly before. It feels different so I'm hopeful." Sophia nodded while looking for confirmation from her colleagues.

There were several nods while Samuel, true to character, remained still and non-committal.

Laura referred them back to the flipchart list and said: "So, this all started with me asking you the question 'HOW will you hold each other accountable?'" I suggest you now discuss and agree how you will keep this open and honest dialogue going, keep it alive, when you're back at work?"

A lively discussion followed where the team kicked ideas around and finally found themselves united in agreement.

Laura leapt to the flipchart and started scribbling with great energy. Now the mood was vibrant, there was an absolute buzz in the air. She could even notice a difference in the way people were sitting; some were on the edge of their seats, some leaning forward and some getting decidedly animated.

Based on the team's input, this is what she wrote:

HOW TO HOLD EACH OTHER ACCOUNTABLE – how we do it

- ✓ Check what commitments we've made and how we're doing against them
- ✓ Regular follow-up on agreements in our meetings
- ✓ Check-in on how everyone is doing in our meetings
- ✓ Learn to give and receive feedback more effectively
- ✓ Give each other regular feedback

Emboldened by their progress, the team got on a roll and steamed through the rest of the list of findings. They realised that the only way to address their findings was to work as a tight team in co-creating the solutions, having agreement by everyone to ensure buy-in.

Inwardly, Laura reflected on the first day.

"What do they implicitly know and what do I need to explicitly explain about what we've done today and what they've gained? Do they all understand what they've experienced so they can make full use of it?"

The clock on the mantelpiece let out five soft chimes, Laura started to summarise the day:

"You've made great progress as a team today, so well done!" To make sure they'd absorbed her words, Laura looked at each of them deliberately. She had their full attention.

"You've been genuinely open in your conversations. This is critical behaviour for a successful team. And now that you've started this, you have to continue it. It will get easier and easier and you will get better and better at it. It's a skill and a habit that you can take with you wherever you go, personally and professionally. When you talk openly and respectfully, you break down barriers and you get to results quicker. Frankly you can't afford not to do it."

She paused for effect. They were all quiet and Laura could imagine the cogwheels turning, slow at first and then picking up speed as the message sunk in.

Comfortable that the team had taken on her message, she continued.

"You've made some commitments and we will continue this work tomorrow and get more specific. You've started to build a foundation of trust and you will need to continue building that if you want to be successful. You are no longer purely individuals in a group; you are team members relying on each other, having had a shift in mindset after today's disclosures. That's how bonds are created in a team. You are all in this together."

"We're done here for today" she continued. "Tonight I have a surprise for you and all your team skills will be required to get through it." She smiled like someone who had a secret. She knew that she'd made them curious, in a good way.

Chapter 19: Which way now?

"All for one, one for all, that is our device."

Alexandre Dumas

The team was assembled on the wide stone steps leading away from the hotel. Their curiosity was palpable. Framing the steps were two stone ornaments in the shape of acorns, a reflection of the many oak trees present in the hotel grounds.

Without any preamble, Laura led them down the stairs, waving her hand with a 'follow-me' gesture.

Walking through the garden towards the back of the hotel, JR and Sophia walked closely together. Sophia giggled at something JR had just said, as he leaned down towards her. The others walked in silence, wondering what surprise Laura had up her sleeve. Christine felt tired and was grateful that they were finally outside in the fresh air. It had been an energy-draining day, but a good one. Part of her wished she could have had some time to herself, maybe gone for a solitary walk along the river, but she knew that she needed to be with the others; that was the purpose of being here after all.

The sun was low in the sky now and from its warm light the trees cast long shadows across the freshly-mowed lawn. Stephen enjoyed the smell of the newly-cut grass, he always had. It brought back memories of the beautifully manicured lawns that his father always seemed busy maintaining. He smiled at the recollection and was brought back by a shriek of laughter from Sophia. He glanced at her and noted that she and JR seemed to have become very good friends. *"That's nice"* he thought.

Laura walked briskly ahead of them, turning around to make sure that they were all keeping up with her.

Within a few minutes they found themselves standing in front of a tall dark green hedge, neatly trimmed with leaves so shiny they looked like they had been polished. There was a perfect archway in the middle of the hedge.

"A garden maze! What on earth are we doing here?" thought Samuel. He felt apprehensive. *"I hate mazes, they're stupid and pointless!"*

Laura smiled at the team of six in front of her.

"What is this?" She pointed towards the archway.

A chorus of "a maze" was the response.

"That's right. What do you know about mazes?"

Samuel was quick to share his knowledge: "Mazes are believed to originate from Egypt and Greece, some 4000 years ago. Their purpose might have been to keep unwelcome visitors out. They are often linked to paganism and were seen as mystical." He enjoyed how superior this made him feel. He felt like he reclaimed some power after having been challenged earlier on.

"That's interesting" JR admitted "I had no idea they were that old."

"I have to confess that I don't like mazes. When I was on a school trip I got lost in a maze for almost an hour. It was horrible and I've avoided them ever since." The confession was Anna's.

"So tell us Laura, why are we standing here by this maze?" Stephen was genuinely intrigued; Laura had not briefed him on this.

Laura suddenly looked more serious as she replied: "You will learn the secret of the maze tonight. This maze has many blind alleys and dead ends. It can take a very long time to go through the maze, you might get lost, need to backtrack, or you could fast track through it by finding the most direct route. That is your challenge. That is your team task. I will give you your instructions only once, so please listen carefully".

They all did.

"You will enter the maze here. Your team task is to find the shortest route through the maze. You will be given tasks along the way. If you carry out the tasks correctly, you will be shown the shortest way. Good luck! See you on the other side."

She turned on her heels, and took off in the opposite direction, simultaneously waving her mobile phone in the air.

"Why is she doing that with her phone?" asked Anna to no one in particular.

"I have no idea, but I'm sure we'll find out. She's obviously up to something" Sophia said.

"So, what do we do now?" asked Anna, looking at Stephen.

"I guess we go in" he said "I don't know any more than you do. Let's just go. The quicker we do this, the quicker we can have dinner".

Stephen led the way through the archway and they soon found themselves dwarfed by the hedges lining their path. There was a density to the foliage that made it impossible to see through it. It almost felt like being in a box; to the left and right there were hedges and straight ahead was another hedge where the path turned at a 90-degree angle. The path, only wide enough for two, was a dusty pale grey. The evening sun could not reach into the maze, and it suddenly felt much darker than it had done outside it. After a few bends, they had already lost their sense of direction.

"Where are we going? Which way are we heading? Where are we trying to get to?" Anna asked with a hint of nerves in her voice.

"Well, so far we haven't come to any crossroads so I guess we just keep going" Christine suggested. As soon as she'd said that, they turned another corner and the narrow track split into three. To the right of the junction was a plaque. JR spotted it first and walked up to it. An envelope with Stephen's name on it was attached to the top of the plaque. JR peeled off the tape and handed the envelope to Stephen. They were all watching keenly as he turned it over and flipped open the fold.

"We've got to be quick; we need to get through this maze as quickly as we can". Sophia was impatient.

"Hold on" countered Christine "I don't think Laura said we just had to get through as fast as possible. Did she?"

"No, you're right. She said that we need to find the shortest, most direct route" JR confirmed. "What's in the envelope?" All eyes were on Stephen again.

Meanwhile, Stephen had read the message given to him and he now looked puzzled.

"You read it to the others. I need to think" Stephen said to Samuel.

Samuel was surprised and secretly pleased. He put on an air of importance as he unfolded the sheet of paper.

He read:

> Stephen, what is the biggest mistake you've made as a leader, and what did you learn from it? Please share with your team.
>
> Then Anna must call this number and explain Stephen's answer AND what she learned from that answer.

Anna looked startled, but kept quiet.

Without consciously knowing it, they all shifted closer together. Stephen paced up and down the track, his hand against his forehead in a thinker's pose. He repeated the question under his breath, searching for the answer. The others watched him, not quite sure what to say.

Eventually Stephen stopped and said: "I've got it".

"When I first became a leader, I threw myself into that role with a lot of energy and ideas of how to manage a team. It went well for a while, until an organisational change was announced. The change would affect my team and I needed to communicate all of this to them, so I called a meeting and laid out the facts in a rational, logical fashion. I really thought I was doing it the right way."

"So what happened?"

"Well, I think I need to explain the change in question. My team had previously all been working in a regular 9 to 5 work pattern, but now they would be required to work one evening a week until 8pm to cater for the extended customer service proposition the company had identified was needed. I didn't think it was such a big deal, as people would actually be getting a raise to make up for the inconvenience of working out of regular office hours. I totally underestimated the impact on them. "

"What was the impact then?"

"I thought I'd done my job, I wrapped up the meeting and was ready to move on to the next thing" Stephen brushed his palms up and down in a scissor-like movement, indicating he had brushed off the task.

"I was wrong. It wasn't done, it wasn't finished. One of my most outspoken team members bellowed out:

"I can't believe you've just dropped that bomb shell on us and expect that to be that. Do you have any idea how difficult this will be for some of us? We have other

commitments outside of work and if we are supposed to work one evening a week, this affects our families, friends and our personal life. I don't know how I am going to do this! Can you even do this to us? What about our legal rights? I didn't sign up for this!"

"I can still feel that cold lump in my stomach, which came from a sudden sense of embarrassment. How could I have overlooked this impact on them? I had been so busy just getting on with it, wanting to complete the task that had been given to me, that I had truly forgotten about the effect on the people in question."

Stephen let out a slow sigh of relief, as he became aware that he had never really talked about this properly to anyone. It felt surprisingly good. He took a step back and looked at the others who were staring back at him, clearly hanging on his every word.

"So what did you do?" JR's question came out very quickly.

"I wasn't ready for that reaction, so I tried to gloss over it and stumbled over my words. I somehow managed to close the meeting, saying that I would come back to them on their concerns. It seemed a feeble response, even to me, but to be brutally honest, it was all I was capable of doing. Now that was a mistake, the whole thing was a mistake. After I made my escape, I shut myself in my office and started replaying events in my head to figure out where it had gone wrong and what to do next. Meanwhile my team was outside, probably talking about me and what a horrible meeting we'd had and how badly I had handled it."

The words were gushing out of Stephen now; it was as if a tap had been turned on.

"To cut a long story short, I spent the next weeks and months making up for the trust I had lost. I'll never do that again. It taught me a lesson about how to communicate change, and that nothing is ever as straightforward as it seems on paper. I didn't take into account how people would feel about the change and that will always be more important than the mere facts."

As Stephen uttered the words, he was almost in slow motion as, inside his head, the penny fully dropped. "Ah, of course" he mumbled to himself.

It was quiet; apart from a faint tweeting of a bird that seemed to have joined the crowd, sitting on top of the hedge.

Samuel started fidgeting with some loose change in his pocket, bringing them all back to the moment.

"Wow! Thank you for telling us that story. That can't have been easy to talk to us about." Sophia patted Stephen appreciatively on the arm, looking him straight in the eye.

"You know what, by talking about it, I've had some new insights. That was unexpected." Stephen trailed off into his own thoughts.

"Great, now let's make that call. Anna, what did you learn from the example?" Christine turned to face Anna.

Anna didn't respond straight away, she was still thinking. When she had come to clarity in her mind, she said: "It was fascinating to see how you, Stephen, gained so much yourself by sharing the story out loud. I very rarely do that myself as I tend to keep my thoughts to myself but maybe, just maybe, I should do this more".

JR nodded encouragingly. Samuel looked uncomfortable and distant, staring at the hedge.

Anna picked up her phone and resolutely tapped in the phone number they had been given. Within two rings, Laura had answered.

"It's Laura" Anna mouthed to the others.

She then turned her attention back to the phone and explained what they had talked about in an energetic way. She was rewarded by a "well done" from Laura and told that they had performed their task to her satisfaction. She gave Anna the clue; the shortest route was the one to the left.

Anna punched her fist in the air, saying "yes" and the others cheered.

"We've been told the shortest route; it's this one, let's go!" exclaimed Anna and started for the option furthest to the left. The others followed closely behind.

The maze continued to embrace them in its dark green cloak as they darted down the route they had been shown.

A few minutes later they stood at yet another crossroad. There was another plaque on the side with an envelope, just like at their last stop, and on it read: 'Samuel'. JR was the first to reach the plaque, he handed the envelope to Samuel.

Samuel clearly showed his disdain for the whole exercise by reluctantly getting the folded paper out and turning away from the others as he read its message. They heard him sigh.

"I'm not doing this" he said brusquely. "No-one is going to tell me what I should or shouldn't talk about. I say we try out the different routes; we can do it together or take turns going down different routes. We can keep in contact over the mobiles. What do you say?"

His bold statement was met by surprise. Christine reflected on the fact that she knew Samuel wasn't a team player, but that she had somehow expected him to get in line for this and just play by the rules. "Obviously not" she thought to herself. He had been getting on her nerves for a long time but now she noticed how her annoyance had subsided slightly. Inwardly she shrugged Samuel's behaviour off. She decided that she didn't want him to have the power to make her annoyed.

Stephen gave Samuel a brief grin and said: "Come on, Samuel, we all need to do this. How bad can the question be?" he attempted a joking tone.

"It's not about that. I just think there are different ways of getting to the same result. Let's explore the different routes." Samuel would not be swayed. "That's the end of that. You can't make me do anything." He looked defiantly at Stephen, ignoring the rest.

"Very well" said Stephen "let's do it your way, but be prepared to get lost and seriously delayed." His annoyance was on display but he didn't care.

Sophia was about to throw herself into an attempt to convince Samuel to reconsider, but decided against it. *"Let him dig himself into a hole"* she thought and remained quiet.

They split into pairs: JR with Sophia, Samuel with Anna and Stephen with Christine. They set off down their appointed paths in silence. No-one was impressed.

It only took Samuel and Anna a short time to get lost in the copious dead ends and blind alleys. Anna had never had a good sense of direction and felt thoroughly confused and scared. Her frustration turned into anger, which she tried hard to suppress.

"Where are we? Where the BEEP are we trying to get to? Why couldn't he just answer the question and why did I get stuck with him?"

Anna's thoughts were interrupted by the sound of muffled voices through the hedge. She recognised Stephen and Christine's dulcet tones and said: "Where are you? We are lost." Samuel frowned. He didn't like to admit that he was lost.

Christine replied, tilting her head back as if talking to the top of the maze: "We're lost too, but we have started to backtrack, trying to remember our route back."

It felt weird not being able to see each other and yet obviously being close enough to talk.

"We're going to go back, keeping to the right" explained Stephen. "What will you do?" talking to the same spot at the top of the maze as Christine had done.

Samuel dismissed him with: "You do that. We will find our own way".

Exasperated, Stephen threw his hands in the air and sped off.

"See you soon" he shouted over his shoulder.

After 10 minutes of co-operation Christine and Stephen found themselves back at the second plaque and were greeted by Sophia and JR who looked very pleased with themselves.

In a hushed voice, Sophia whispered: "We found the right path! But we don't want to tell Samuel, because we've talked about it and we think he should answer the question. So what do you think?"

"Let's not tell him" Christine added. Stephen looked hesitant but then nodded slowly. "OK then, I'll go along with that."

They had to wait another five minutes until they heard Anna approach, stomping her feet angrily. She was ahead of Samuel who was hanging his head as if defeated.

Anna twisted around and, fists on her hips, she finally vented her frustration on Samuel: "You have wasted so much of our time, and I mean all of our time", doing a sweeping gesture to include the others. "You could have just answered the question. We've been lost out there for too long and I hated it. "

"Well, while we were waiting for you, we decided that this is your chance to show that you're a member of this team, Samuel. So we want you to answer the question. We know the route but we are not going to tell you. So there."

Samuel was getting tired and hungry. He decided it wasn't worth fighting anymore.

"How can I give an answer to the question without giving too much away? At least I can take control over that." Samuel pondered.

Samuel threw the paper at Anna and said: "You read it".

Anna read, with a slight smirk on her face:

> Samuel, when did you last feel powerless at work? What did you learn from the experience? Please share with your team.
>
> Then JR must call this number and explain Samuel's answer AND what he, JR, learned from that answer.

"I can't really think of anything. I don't really know that I have ever felt powerless. It's a very American word anyway. We wouldn't say that, would we?" He glanced at his fellow Brit for acknowledgement.

"It doesn't really matter, you know what it means." Stephen said impatiently.

Samuel rolled his eyes and continued, "I guess I would feel powerless if one of my direct reports went to Stephen with an issue, instead of coming straight to me. That wouldn't make me feel very powerful. OK. Are you happy with that?"

"Has that actually happened then, and what did you learn?" Anna asked.

"Well yes, it did happen."

"So what did you learn?" Anna poked.

In a fake, exaggerated voice, Samuel said "What I learned was to keep a closer eye on my people". He gave a half-grin and then added in his normal voice "and that it helps if I'm more accessible".

JR shook his head in disbelief and picked up the phone without commenting. When Laura answered, JR explained what Samuel had said and then added: "People are annoyed here. I learned that you can make it hard for yourself or you can make it easy, and we've just gone through a long-winded process that was stupidly difficult, which it really didn't need to be. If we're all in it together, we all need to play. That's what I learned. "

"Good learning, JR" said Laura "but unfortunately as a team you have failed the task. The level of sharing wasn't up to the standard of the first one. I'm afraid I can't give you your clue. "

JR put down the phone and broke the news to the others: "No clue from Laura. The sharing wasn't deep enough to convince her that we had completed the task. "

A brief silence was followed by Sophia's exclamation: "We know the way, let's just go".

They were getting used to their green surroundings and although the last stop had soured the atmosphere, they were strangely comfortable in the maze. There was now a level of familiarity with the tasks; they knew how to win after the first task and they'd just learned how to fail and what that felt like.

At the third plaque, Christine answered her question quickly and openly so they were soon on their way again, able to progress through the maze via the shortest route. Over the last three stops, the team picked up speed as they truly let their guard down and the exchange of experience flowed freely.

Finally, over two hours after they had entered the maze, they spilled out through the final archway, whooping and congratulating each other.

Laura watched them from the wrought-iron bench where she was sitting. She smiled at their exuberance and mused at how powerful this exercise had proven to be. She was always amazed at how well this worked, even though each unique team had its own unique experience.

She walked over to the team. "Good job. It's high time for dinner. Let's head over to the dining room. We'll recap tomorrow when you've had a chance to reflect on the secrets of the maze."

They didn't waste any time in racing off to dinner, they were famished.

Stephen's journal

Has it only been one day?!

It feels like we've been here for much longer. What a day! We've talked more openly in these few hours than I have ever talked to any colleagues or direct reports in my life. What's more, it feels just fine! I have never felt safe talking so candidly to others. I feel as if I know this group so much better than I thought was possible or was even needed. But boy is it needed! We've climbed a massive mountain today.

The challenge of Samuel remains though. We challenged him today and he had to get in line, but I doubt it made a big difference in his outlook. I hope I am wrong, I hope he is having some of the same 'aha' moments that I and the others are having, even if he isn't showing it.

The brain and the body have had their fair share of exercise today, I will sleep well tonight.

Chapter 20: Learning from the Maze

"Learning never exhausts the mind."

Leonardo da Vinci

The room felt lighter on the morning of the second day. Even the illuminated glass-fronted bookcases seemed more brightly lit.

The semi-circle of chairs had been turned around and they were now facing the window, the dark wooden window frames formed a stark contrast to the bright light. The maroon leather upholstery on the heavy armchairs had been worn and softened by time. *"Some things definitely get better with time"*, reflected Samuel.

The crystal chandelier hanging from the middle of the ceiling became more prevalent as they now faced this way. Perhaps this added to the light feeling. The tear-shaped crystal droplets seemed to reflect the light and cascade it around the room. The subtle smell of old wood enhanced the room's historical character.

A brown Encyclopaedia Britannica volume of considerable age caught Anna's gaze. It was bigger than the other books and seemed to stand out. The spine was broken and the cover was torn.

"These old places all have secret passages. What if that is one of them? What would happen if I touched that book? Would the wall fall back to reveal a secret staircase?"

Without even thinking about it, she put her hand out to try it, but was stopped in mid-air as JR bounded into the room. His grin seemed wider than usual.

"Morning, guys!"

It was another lovely, bright day and the green leaves, not yet touched by autumn, were swaying and bouncing in the wind. A hanging basket, overflowing with a plethora of flowers in different colours, was on the perimeter of Laura's view. She pushed away the image from her mind; it was time to start.

"Good Morning everyone" said Laura with a huge smile, "How are we all today?"

With a mixture of nods and smiles around the room the team settled into the session, wondering what was in store today after yesterday's wealth of learning.

Laura carried on. "Yesterday when we started I asked you how you felt coming into this team session and I asked you to share that, do you remember? I want to ask you the same today, before we debrief on the team maze."

There was silence for a moment or two. It was a different kind of silence to the day before. It was clear this time that the team where thinking more deeply about how they felt than they had done yesterday. *"That is interesting in itself."* thought Laura.

"I feel good and am keen to talk about the maze. I enjoyed yesterday and I personally learned a lot" Anna was the first to open up.

"I got more than I thought from our session so I am happier going into today. I was not sure if this team stuff was going to be very beneficial for us but I can see that we have already learned more about each other. It also feels different in this room today, better, closer. I didn't expect that" JR followed Anna.

Stephen nodded his agreement. "I am looking forward to today and getting some feedback from everyone. Yesterday was great for me."

Laura raised her chin towards Sophia. "And you Sophia, how do you feel?"

"Yep, good, although to be honest I am feeling a little apprehensive about today. Now I know a bit more about what we are doing, I am wondering what is ahead of us. I admit we did move further as a team yesterday, we had some tough moments and once we got through those tough moments it felt better. It's as if we know each other better; I feel we have built some more trust with each other. Can that be true?" She questioned the team.

Christine was quick to react. "Yes I think so, I feel more comfortable with you all today". Her eyes glanced at Samuel as she said 'all'. "I want this team to work better together and I think the team climate study yesterday got all the issues out on the table. We had some good ideas and I want to see them followed through."

Samuel slowly looked around the room. Everyone had spoken except for him and he was receiving a few hard stares from his colleagues. He was beginning to realise that he wasn't going to get away with being silent anymore; so for him, yes, things in the team had changed. If Sophia was apprehensive he was VERY apprehensive but he contemplated what he was going to say very carefully.

"I am OK and I want to get on with today."

Laura looked at Samuel and decided to leave it there for now, she knew he was going to get a lot of feedback in a minute; she didn't need to probe him any further. She launched into explaining what they had been doing.

"Yesterday you spent time with each other working on HOW you operate as a team. The key to this is spending time together, focusing on what is important to you as a team. This begins to deepen the trust levels. You already have a degree of trust and with teams we are always working on increasing those levels of trust. When we build trust it allows us to work more closely together, understanding why you rely on each other, to break down the silos and become more efficient. In today's world it is even more important to pull together, share resources and work smarter together, not always harder."

Laura paused to check she had their attention.

"Spending time together and sharing has helped you to open up and create a greater sense of team. In the team climate study you worked on a number of areas for you to develop, as well as those you know are your strengths. Utilising what you are good at and sharing this across the team will help you with your developments.   Yesterday you also said you wanted and needed to work on trust as a team. The team maze also helped you to learn more about each other and to see how you deal with a team task."

"Why do we need to spend time together to build trust?" Christine questioned Laura.

"Well, you probably spend time together at the moment but you don't talk about the things we are covering here. You talk about tasks, to do lists, tactics and actions. You clearly need to do that to run the business. When we spend time getting to know each other it allows us to take time on relationships and building these relationships. This means we know each other better, which starts to form the basis for a stronger relationship, which builds trust. It simply makes us feel better about who we work with and more comfortable with them.

You cannot say 'at 4.30pm today we will work on trust', it is more complex than that and always happens at a behavioural level. It has to be intrinsic in what you are doing, just like it was yesterday for us."

There were some giggles around the room as they smiled at the 4.30pm comment. Laura felt this was a great opportunity to move into the team maze discussion. She was looking forward to this and some straight talking.

"Sooo, how did you find the exercise in the maze? Did you find the secrets of the maze?" Laura, exaggerating for effect, was eager to get the team talking about what they had experienced.

Silence again. There was something about the maturity of the room that made it feel timeless, almost like time stood still there. It created a sense of comfort and safety, which was Laura's intention and one of the reasons why Laura had picked this particular room. The room and the setting were always important when getting teams together and getting team members to open up. The environment was critical and this one was perfect.

"How do you want to do this?" Sophia asked Laura.

"Well thanks Sophia," Laura smiled, "let me give you some questions to think about." She stood up and moved to the flipchart where she turned over a page to reveal some thought provoking questions for them to focus on. The list read:

DEBRIEF OF THE MAZE EXERCISE

1. What was it like being in the maze?
2. What did you do well as a team during the team exercise, what do you feel proud of?
3. What did you not do so well during the team exercise, what do you feel frustrated by?
4. How does this apply to your team when you are back in the workplace? What parallels can you make?
5. Anything else?

The team gazed up at the flipchart. Stephen picked up his notebook. He had clearly made some notes on his observations and was preparing to get them out. Anna already had her notepad on her knee; she had been twiddling her pen between her finger and thumb while they were talking. They had taken the time overnight to reflect; now they were ready to talk.

Christine started "Well I think we did complete the task of getting through the maze but it wasn't the quickest way and we didn't work that well together to get to the end result. Sometimes we got the clues and sometimes we didn't. I got very frustrated at certain points."

Anna jumped in. "I think it was very clever the way you made us do the exercises with the envelopes. I really liked that, it felt good to hear people's stories and I was surprised that I could pick up things for myself from hearing other people talk. For example, Christine I didn't know that you found it so hard to talk to us and come back to us after dinner that time when you got upset in the archipelago. I think we didn't support and recognise how hard it was for you. I think as a team we should have been more sensitive to you and showed you more support. Thanks for sharing that with us. It is a good example of what builds trust as I feel our relationship is better because you told us about that."

"Thanks Anna" Christine gave a small smile then continued, she took a deep breath in, "but what about you Samuel? I found it very frustrating in the maze when you just wouldn't answer the question, why did you do that?"

Laura intervened "Christine, tell us how you felt at that moment?"

"How did I feel? I felt angry and I felt let down. I couldn't believe that you just wouldn't do that simple task for us as a team."

Anna continued, following Christine, "I think that was my lowest point in the maze, when I felt like just giving up. You made me feel like you are just not one of us and you don't want to be. Do you actually want to be in this team?" She appeared angry and was rushing her words. She had had enough.

"Well now that you mention it, I think you were just like you are at work". Sophia pointed at the flipchart. "It says here: 'How does this apply to your team when you are back in the workplace?' Well back at work you really don't appear to be one of us. You ignore our emails and don't respond to us."

The tension in the room was rising. Stephen was sitting on the edge of his seat, he knew this was going to come out into the open but it had happened quicker than he expected. Clearly it had upset people more than he had realised. He looked to Laura for guidance. Should he step in? Laura looked away, letting the comments sink in.

JR shook his head in despair. Samuel slumped lower into his chair. He could not wiggle out of this one. He was aware that his refusal to answer the question, and his insistence that they find their own way through the maze, seemed to have upset everyone. It seemed ridiculous now, why had he done that? *"It would have been easier to just answer the question"* he thought.

"Well, I thought we should use our initiative in the maze and find our own way out. I can see why you think it wasn't quicker but really we did find a quicker way but you were not all in agreement. I am a part of this team and I am here with you so that makes me a team member" Samuel was speaking very quietly and the others were straining to hear him, he looked uneasy.

"I guess that is as good as we can expect from you for now" said JR in what seemed to be a very loud voice compared to Samuel's.

Stephen wondered if he should say something now. He decided to leave it as the team were putting pressure on Samuel. It was good as it felt like the team was dealing with it, not only Stephen.

Stephen wanted to talk more about other aspects of the maze. "I really enjoyed the maze exercise even though I didn't expect to. I didn't like the feeling of not knowing where we were going and not being able to see where we were heading. I guess that is just like in business; I like to know where we are heading. I felt lost when we couldn't see the end point, it was confusing. Maybe that is something we should talk about as a team? Do we all know where we are heading? I think we are going to cover that today, aren't we Laura?" He looked over at Laura who slowly moved her head up and down.

Stephen continued, "It felt great when we got to the end of the maze. We had achieved our task together, as a team. I liked that, it was as if we had all got together behind something and made it happen. I guess this is what happens at work when we have a crisis and we all pull together. We should do this more, even when there is not a crisis. We are a good team and we really can pull together. More importantly, it felt good when we did. I also enjoyed learning all about each other. The questions were very revealing." He stopped and decided to add one last comment to show his team how he felt, "I too felt frustrated when Samuel did not answer his question."

Laura stood up and moved to the centre of the room, she was taking back control of the discussion. She wanted to capture the results of their learning and then move onto the part of the session where they would give each other feedback in a structured way: The giving and receiving feedback exercise. Laura knew this would pull out all that was needed for the team and, moreover, it would be done in an effective and safe way.

She recapped on their learning; they all chipped in to create the lists. Laura was happily scribbling them onto the flipchart pages, the answers came very easily from the team now. They poured out their learning for Laura to capture. They seemed keen to get it in writing and to work on solutions. Laura often found that teams were very keen on getting to solutions once they had gone through the tough learning and difficult conversations. Laura always had to ensure they didn't rush to solutions without first having the conflict that was often needed.

The lists read:

Team Maze - Feel proud of

- Hearing people's personal stories was great – learnt a lot, got to know each other deeper, built trust
- Good questions to ask each other – we should use these at other times and spend time doing that as a team as well as our normal team meetings
- Improved our relationships – we had to solve something together and share, that was good
- To do something and achieve it together as a team felt good – let's do that more

- We do pull together in a crisis – could we pull together at other times like that, not just in a crisis?

Frustrated by

- Not the quickest way out of the maze because we didn't pull together and gain team agreement. How often do we do that and cause rework and more work in the office that affects profitability and the bottom line?
- We could have shown each other more support at times – seemed to be working in silos, like in the office, again that is affecting our bottom line
- Feeling frustrated when Samuel would not answer the question, felt like he doesn't want to be in the team – that has an effect on all of us – we all need to be a team
- Not knowing what direction we are headed in – not knowing where we are going as a team
- Dead ends and blind alleys felt frustrating – do we create those at work by not communicating?

Laura wrapped up: "This is good work, well done, later today we will pull all of this together with your other learning from the 2 days. We will agree your commitments and how you can apply all of this as part of your team formula and keep it alive. Now, I think it is time for a break, let's meet back here in 17 minutes."

The team left the room and spilled out into the beautiful sunny day.

Chapter 21: TOP feedback

"People can't change the truth but the truth can change people."

Unknown

The sun was glistening on the river as Laura sat, observing the team. There was laughter coming from them and a steady banter; they seemed more at ease with each other. For the first time, Samuel stayed with the team for coffee; he usually spent the breaks on his own and would always be the last to return to the room.

Once back in the room, JR noticed a second door. It was the first time he had noticed it, hidden amongst the books with a big brass door knob. He wondered what was on the other side. What would he discover if he opened the door? He recognised that the team were about to open the door to their next discovery. What would they discover now?

Laura wanted to get straight into it so she explained to the team that they were going into a feedback exercise. She proceeded to explain the exercise and how it would work.

"We are going to give each other some feedback, this is very important in teams. Why do you think that is?" she asked the team.

The team members were getting better at responding and JR was the first.

"I think it is very important that we all understand how we are perceived. I think I know how I am seen, but I sure would like some thoughts from others to confirm that, or let me know otherwise."

"I want to know how I am doing and I want to hear from others what they think. Surely we all need to have that?" Sophia said.

"I would really like to see if I have any blind spots; something that others can see that I can't, that is always helpful, isn't it?" Anna added with a nervous laugh.

"I think we should give feedback but I really don't like the idea of it. I am not sure." Christine was nervous.

"I am really keen to hear what you all think. I believe it will help us as a team." Stephen was sitting on the edge of his seat again.

Laura stood up again enthusiastically. "These are all really good reasons. As a team, once again, this process will allow you to understand each other and further build trust, as well as getting to know how you are perceived."

"I would like you to think about each member of this team carefully in turn, and think about the feedback you would like to give them, feedback that will help and support them. This is an opportunity for you to reflect back to them what you have seen them do and say. This is helpful because it's often difficult, if not impossible, for people to do it themselves. Feedback is one of the key components of the team formula. It is simple but to be effective you need to keep the feedback at a *behavioural* level, not a task level."

Laura had reached the 'make or break' moment that could revolutionise this team. She had experienced this so many times before. She knew that this was it. The structure always worked. Now it was time to explain it to them.

"Let's look at it", she said and exposed another flipchart paper, showing the 'TOP feedback' formula.

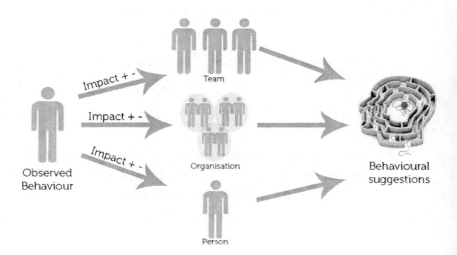

"The 'TOP feedback' formula shows how you first think about the person's behaviours, which you have observed. You then consider what IMPACT you think those behaviours have on the **T**eam, the **O**rganisation and finally on you **P**ersonally, with a specific focus on how it makes you feel. In our experience, that personal emotional impact is what helps people realise the effect they have on others more than anything else. That creates transformational change rather than just intellectual understanding. It helps people to *really* get it, deep down. The final component of the formula is your suggestion for what they could do going forward. Keep in mind that this could, and of course should, also be reinforcements of what is already working well, if you have observed a powerful behaviour in someone that you want to reinforce." Every member of the team had their eyes riveted on the flipchart, engrossed in the formula. They were captivated by the potential that it held.

Laura now gave them their task: "You have an hour to go away and prepare this feedback formula for each of your team members. Do you have any questions?"

"How will it work when we come back? Who will start?" Christine was concerned.

"When we get started, we will go around the room and let everyone give their feedback to the same person. So if we were to start with Anna, for example, each of you would share all of your feedback for her with her." Laura clarified.

Christine acknowledged the answer with a slow nod and they all got up to leave.

Outside the door, they scattered in different directions. Stephen walked purposefully through the main doors and headed towards the bench by the maze. He settled down and glanced at the maze through the corner of his eye. What had happened there last night had been a metaphor for how this team functioned, especially the roles they each played in it. Being close to the maze seemed to help him crystallise his thoughts:

"The level of disclosure in my feedback will set the tone. The others will model what I do, so I need to make sure my feedback is both factual and personal. I do realise that, and Laura has very clearly pointed that out to me too. How I receive their feedback to me will also matter greatly. They may have feedback for me that is tough for me to hear, but if I'm defensive then that may stop them from giving me the feedback and I really want to know what impact I'm having. I am beginning to understand, on a whole new level, why this is so important. If I want to be a great leader, I have to know and take control of my impact."

Back in the room Anna was sitting quietly, she had gone to look for a place to sit but after walking across the lawn to the river and taking in some fresh air, she had decided to return to the library. In this great room she may get some inspiration as it was packed with the beautifully bound books and there was a wealth of knowledge here. Laura was the only other person in the room, she was just sitting reading. Anna scribbled on her notepad, jotting down her thoughts on the other members of the team. She was really focusing on all the great behaviours she had noticed in them. Somehow she found it easier to think of all the positives first. Anna was thinking very carefully about how she was going to say this to the team. She was wondering what it would be like to give this feedback, her mind started wandering off, thinking about what the others where writing about her. She munched at the end of her pen, deep in thought and forced her thoughts back onto her team members.

*

"Let's get started".

It was an hour later and the team were all assembled, seated and ready to go.

"The next part of the process is for us to share the feedback with each other using the 'TOP feedback' formula. I would like you to stay focused on behaviours when giving the feedback. When we give and receive feedback we need to think about some principles. Feedback is a gift, you give it and receive it graciously; thank the person, don't be defensive, and then it is your choice what you do with the feedback. The feedback should contain positive and constructive comments. Without feedback you are flying blind. Remember it is their perception of you and it is given with a positive intent, they are trying to help. Perception is personal as everyone may interpret a situation differently. Perception is not fact, but the perception reflects the impact your behaviour has had on that person. It therefore becomes their reality and that's the impact you have."

"Wow", thought JR to himself. He felt like he had just had an epiphany. *"So there are no absolute truths, only perceptions, and I have to deal with others' perceptions of me and I can choose my response to them. I had not seen it that way before. I'd always believed that I have to change what I do when someone gives me feedback, and as I sometimes get differing feedback, I don't always know what to do. This has helped me understand that I need to focus on HOW I do what I do, focus on my behaviours, to effectively influence people's perception of me. Now I get it!"*

Their eyes were eagerly fixed on Laura as the focal point in the room. When they had arrived back into the room she had asked them to pull their chairs in to close the circle, moving it from a semi-circle of chairs to a small circle. It was as if the room had just got smaller. It felt different, this had already changed the dynamics and once again it was even more intense. Christine smiled nervously at Stephen, her face a little flushed.

"I want to get going", JR boomed out. He was bouncing his knee up and down in an energetic way, causing the others to look down at his impatient gesture.

"Are we ready? OK then, who wants to receive feedback first?" asked Laura.

Without any hesitation Samuel raised his hand in a classroom style, much to the surprise of those around him. "I want to go first".

"Right, now remember the 'TOP Feedback' formula" Laura waved her hand towards the flipchart to her right. "Off we go. Who would like to give Samuel his feedback to begin?"

Sophia's eyes darted towards JR.

"Well Samuel," JR started "I want to give you my *gift*". Some of the team giggled at his emphasis on the word gift. He had clearly found it amusing to think of feedback as a gift. When the nervous laughter had settled down, JR continued.

"What I really like about you Samuel is the amount of knowledge that you have of this business and of this organisation. It has an impact on the team because we have access to you; you can help us to figure out a way around some of the issues we face. You know who to go to if we need help to get something done. I would like to see you do more of it though." He took a sideways glance at the formula.

"For the organisation, you are very experienced and that is incredibly valuable. For me personally, I am comfortable with your level of understanding of our business and asking you to help me out. Once again, I would like more of it and I would like you to volunteer that rather than me always having to ask you for it. The impact on the team is that I don't feel you are a part of it and you don't really support us. I would like you to feel more a part of this team. To the organisation we don't appear to have a united front as I am never sure how you will represent us to others."

Once again JR looked at the flipchart to follow the structure.

"To me personally, it is sometimes difficult to work with you because you are not very forthcoming. You don't volunteer information or share with us, you don't seek us out. I therefore avoid working with you, which is not good for the team, the organisation or me. I think we could make more of an impact on the results if we worked together better. What I would like you to do is to get involved more, share more with us and show support for us, as a team, to other areas of the business. That's it."

He threw his hands in the air turning his palms upwards as if handing Samuel a gift. The others smiled and there was some more nervous laughter. JR had articulated his perception very well.

Samuel had been looking straight at JR throughout this whole exchange and was now nodding. "Thank you, JR" he said.

"Well Done!" Laura started clapping. "Let's show JR and Samuel our appreciation for going first in this process and for doing it so well." The others joined in with the applause, making a noise that spread across the library and beyond into the hallway outside. They were all surprised at how loud they were clapping, letting out their nervous energy by forcing their hands together.

Sophia was quick to jump in. "I find your level of understanding of this business very good, I like the way you have the ability to make people listen when you talk, you don't say much so when you do it has a real impact. Like JR, I would like you to share more with us. When you do this with this team, we listen to you and we learn from you, but when you don't say anything we don't learn, so please say more. The organisation is also missing out on your experience when you don't talk and tell us what is happening. The impact on me is that I find it frustrating that I always have to come to you for information when you could easily share it with me, so it feels like hard work to work with you. It doesn't need to be. I like your sense of humour; when you decide to use it, it's great, but not many people get to experience it. I would like more of that; it seems like the real Samuel, I would like him to come out more."

Sophia stopped and took a deep breath. The pause caused the rest of the team to become even more attentive, deeper in the circle. She continued.

"You don't always get team alignment. In fact, it sometimes seems like you almost play us off against each other. When we were in the maze you didn't get our agreement, so we were not aligned when you asked us to go off and find our way through the maze. We were not behind that decision, yet you still carried on. It was clear we were not going to succeed."

"So to follow the process, the impact on the team is that we don't feel we can trust you to support us and carry out what we have agreed as a team. To the organisation that just makes our department look like we don't know what we are doing. I believe that we lost that customer because of your lack of sharing information with us. You didn't get our agreement on the actions you took on our behalf. For me personally, I find it difficult to believe that you will do what you say you will do. I want to add that I do like the real Samuel when he comes out and when you let him out; I can have fun with him." She put her head down to look at the floor and sat back in her chair. She seemed pleased that it was over.

Samuel was writing. He looked like he was thinking about what Sophia had been saying, he had raised his right eyebrow into a very high arch when she talked about allowing the *real* Samuel to come out.

"Urr, thank you Sophia. That is really interesting and food for thought." He opened his mouth as if to say more but stopped himself and shook his head, he was working hard at not being defensive. He did so want to justify his actions in that customer case, but realised that Sophia had a point.

The rest of the feedback given to him was similar. Stephen also added his concern with Samuel not sticking to his commitments and how hurtful it had been when Samuel had gone behind his back to Helmut. Stephen also recognised him positively for his experience and how much the team could learn from him.

Laura looked at Samuel and asked: "What was that like?"

"OK, actually", admitted Samuel "much better than I imagined. It's interesting that there were such similar observations of me. There must be some truth in them. It was also more positive than I thought it would be." He looked pleased at this.

"Thanks, Samuel."

It was then Stephen's turn to listen to his feedback.

Anna volunteered this time.

"I'd like to start. The fact that you're doing this team development process for us means that you want what's best for the team. It really demonstrates your commitment. So it's good for us, but it will also be good for the company in the long term. We will be a more cohesive team, working more constructively with other teams, have fewer misunderstandings and get results quicker. Ultimately we will deliver a unique customer experience, which is what we are here for."

Anna hadn't once looked at her notes, showing how genuine and heartfelt her message was.

"For me personally, I am happy to work with you, for all these reasons. I really like feeling part of a team and with you creating this team spirit I feel part of something important and that makes me feel connected and engaged so that I want to do more. I enjoy working for you. On the more constructive side, I think you have avoided some of the issues in the team, such as Samuel breaking our agreement." She looked down into her notes, avoiding the others.

The closeness of the circle meant that everyone looked down, mirroring her body language without thinking about it; this happens when a team becomes more connected.

"It made us talk amongst ourselves rather than with you, it unsettled us. This has distracted us from our work to some degree which has a bad impact on the organisation. And for me, I felt disappointed because I thought I had left that lack of leadership behind when I left my last leader."

There was a pregnant pause.

Stephen nodded to acknowledge her honesty. "Look, I just want to say that I know I did that, and I understand the impact it's had. I take my role as a leader very seriously and I promise that it won't happen again."

"I believe you. I'm behind you, I'm with you. I want to help you make this team work." Anna closed her notebook and put it on the floor.

Stephen wanted to say more but instead he sat back and gently nodded his head.

Samuel raised his hand in a classroom style again.

"I'll go next."

They all straightened their backs as if standing to attention, curious of what Samuel was so eager to say.

"I'm going to be different. I want to start with your development areas. When you make decisions, you involve far too many people. As a leader you should be able to make decisions yourself, show that you've made them, stick to them and stop asking for others' opinions all the time. "

Christine interrupted: "I disagree. The fact that you, Stephen, ask for our opinions makes us feel involved in the decisions, which is what a great leader does. I also believe that we can contribute to better decisions when we share our collective experience."

Samuel waited for Christine to finish, made no acknowledgement of her at all and then simply carried on.

"You have a good understanding of the business and you have an ability to see the bigger picture. I like that." His matter-of-fact statement was direct and brief.

Laura wanted to keep the process on track, so she asked Samuel: "You mentioned Stephen's decision making process.

What is the impact on the team, on the organisation and on you, personally? And how does it make you feel?"

Samuel forced himself to consider the impact. "It takes so much time to make a decision when the whole team is involved. To the organisation, we are just going to be seen as slow to come to decisions, and for me personally, I am frustrated because I have better things to do."

Samuel stopped after his short and direct outburst.

"And the positives, what are they?" Laura asked, again she pointed to the flipchart.

"I think the rest of the team can benefit from your business sense, and it should benefit the customers of course. Personally, I like the way you communicate the bigger picture, as I think in those terms as well. My suggestion is that you continue to keep us updated on the strategy rather than us spending too much time on the nitty-gritty" Samuel finished off.

They carried on sitting in the circle, giving Stephen his feedback with their bodies leaning forward even more now; again they did it in unison without knowing or noticing. Laura liked to observe these dynamics within teams; it never ceased to amaze her, it happened every time.

With all the feedback eventually given, Stephen noted that there were a few key reoccurring themes: that he wanted the best for the team, that he took an interest in people and listened well, that he was good at turning strategies into actionable plans, and that he had not been good at holding people to account.

The morning continued with more great learnings for each person.

Anna was praised for the value she brought to the team through her clear thinking and deep insights. She was pleased to hear that and was pleasantly surprised to find out they wanted her to speak her mind more. On hearing this, Anna felt like she had been given permission to do so.

The feedback for JR told him they all enjoyed his company and how they were often swept away by his enthusiasm. He was also told they wanted him to work less independently and more interdependently as a true team member. He had a strong personality and was great to be around in the team, they needed him. JR hadn't made that connection before.

Christine had some feedback about how well she managed her projects by effectively influencing the people involved. Her main development area was how it could be difficult to work with her when she was negative and that at those times, people tended to avoid her. Christine didn't like hearing this but she knew it was true.

Sophia got very excited about the messages she received. There was much appreciation for her encouraging style and positive outlook. Her impatience was her biggest area to work on as she tended to just drive forward and not consider the finer details and the impact it had on others.

Each member of the team was intensely involved in either giving their colleague their observations or receiving the observations. This meant they felt highly engaged. They were literally on the edge of their seats. They got into the flow of using the 'TOP feedback' formula and after a while it came easily to them: team, organisation, personal level, and then their feelings.

"What a simple yet highly effective way of giving feedback," thought Sophia. *"Often the simple things are the most effective."* She also noticed they had been led very skilfully by Laura. At each stage she had been gently probing them and encouraging them just to say a little more, which had taken them one step further.

Due to the intensity, the hours passed quickly and before they knew it, it was coming up to lunchtime.

"What an amazing achievement! Well done to all of you" said Laura. "How did you find doing that? What was it like?"

"That was great, it was *very* intense but I got so much out of it. I learned a lot about myself and an awful lot about my colleagues. I cannot believe how something so simple can be so revealing. I'm feeling a bit shell shocked right now," Christine declared.

"The level of openness was good and it feels like we shared some things we had never shared before with each other. Is this linked to trust, Laura?" Anna asked.

"Yes Anna, it is very much linked to trust levels. This formula really helps to increase the levels of openness which brings down those barriers and raises the trust. Do you feel you can trust your colleagues more after that exercise?"

"Well yes, it feels very different now in this room, even from yesterday. Is it only yesterday?" she said holding the back of her hand to her forehead, feigning an exhausted look.

The circle had felt like it was getting smaller and smaller throughout the process, almost like they were coming closer together both physically and as a team. *"This is not what I expected"* thought Stephen, *"it was even better"*.

In the following break for lunch, Laura pulled Stephen to the side.

"That went well, didn't it? How do you feel about it?" Laura queried Stephen.

He hesitated. "It was really good, I got more than I expected out of it. My head's spinning though. I'm worn out!"

Laura nodded knowingly. "Yes, that's how most people feel, particularly the leaders. Now, I wanted to catch you as I wanted to share my observations with you."

Stephen looked up, thinking *"no, not more"* but forced himself to invite Laura's insight.

"I'll be direct about this. I have a rhetorical question for you. I don't want an answer, I just want you to go away and think about it."

His eyes locked firmly onto Laura's. He was intrigued.

The warm room was empty apart from them. Laura had clearly waited to catch Stephen out of earshot of the others. Someone had opened the window and he could feel a breeze flowing gently, straight at him. It seemed to slice through the otherwise still room. There was a lingering sense of good energy in the room, which had been created through the openness they had just shared in this very space.

He waited for the question.

Slowly, deliberately, Laura posed her question: "What would this team be like without Samuel in it?" Stephen froze in amazement, Laura continued. "I want you to think about that. Think about the impact it would have on you, the team and the speed at which you could move forward and the kind of results you want and need to be successful."

He didn't know what to say. *"More straight talking"*, he thought.

His awareness was pulled towards the portrait of the young man who had been watching them from above the whole time. The man in the painting had a very serious look on his face and his eyes seemed to bore into Stephen, highlighting the seriousness of the question.

Stephen sighed heavily and exhaled. *"Should I answer the question anyway?"* He thought.

As if Laura could read his mind, she intervened. "As I said, it's a rhetorical question, which you can choose to reflect on. We can talk about this again at some other time if you want."

Stephen felt the urge to respond and opened his mouth, but stopped before any sound could escape from his lips. *"That's a great, great question"* he thought.

"I have a lot to think about. Thank you". Stephen desperately wanted to be on his own, but forced himself to join the team for coffees outside.

Laura watched him leave the room, his shoulders somewhat slumped. She needed some time out; this had been an all-consuming exercise for everyone, including her. Even though this was something Laura did frequently, it was always deeply dynamic. It had to be, to make it a powerful experience.

She found herself by the window, smiling at the sight of children chasing each other, jumping over the flowers, trying to get wet by the water sprinklers. The air was filled with happy shrieks when the water merrily splashed them. She felt encouraged by the simplicity of the play and knew she had been right to put the challenge of the team in simple terms to Stephen.

Chapter 22: A Team of Purpose

"People are motivated through involvement and ownership, to feel they have a say, that they are important and can make a difference. An effective team is not just lead by a leader, it is lead by the whole team, guided and supported by the leader."

They ate lunch outside, warmed by the sun on the patio, and sheltered by a hedge on three sides, the house on the fourth. This meant that even though there was a faint breeze, it had no impact on the temperature at all; it continued to be pleasantly warm like on a midsummer day. It was indeed, in many different ways, a day to remember.

The team was now completely engrossed in the process of becoming a team.

Somehow, any remaining barriers had come down during the feedback exercise. There is something very revealing about feedback, when people truly open up to comments that are given with care and good will. It is often incredibly motivating; people are always surprised at how much positive feedback is included. It makes them feel good and it inspires them. Because they share so much, they are all in it together. They become like the three musketeers, one for all, and all for one.

It was as if Stephen and his team members were only looking for solutions now.

Coming back into the room after lunch, they all seemed high-spirited. Laura noted that they were even a few minutes early, all of them. That was the first time that had happened.

When Laura looked at the animated people in the room, chatting with each other, she was happy for them. She could see and feel an atmosphere of hope. There was relief there too, that she knew. She reflected, *"Most people dread the prospect of feedback, but with the right set-up and careful management, feedback is the main entrance door to learning and excellence. Yet so many people don't dare open it."*

"OK, everyone" said Laura. "We've come to the last main point on our agenda and it's time to use another part of the team formula. We're going to draft up a 'Team Charter'. Do you all know what a Team Charter is?"

The group settled down and turned towards her. She was met by some curious looks.

After consideration, Sophia said: "No. I don't think so." She paused and glanced at her colleagues. "Do you?" The others shook their heads in almost perfect unison.

"Very well" said Laura. "Let me explain. A Team Charter is a document that outlines a team's vision and purpose, goals, roles and responsibilities, operating guidelines and any other relevant aspects to the team's success. It's the outcome of a team brainstorm, discussion and agreement".

A clear Team Charter ensures that everyone is on the same page, going in the same direction, and doing it in such a way that the team is better able to achieve its goals. Our main focus here today is to have you work on your joint vision. I want you to create a visual that encapsulates your vision for the team, the team's purpose, if you like. It will represent what you, as a team, are there to do. How does that sound? How do you feel about that?" Laura waited for a response.

"It sounds brilliant, I like it" said Stephen. "To be honest, I'm not sure we have a shared view of what our purpose is, so I think this will be very, very valuable and interesting to do". He scratched his head with a pensive look.

In the spirit of openness they now shared, he then added: "I haven't considered the importance of this before, as I thought we were all clear on our roles and responsibilities, but I see now that this is something we should have done from the start."

Looking at his team, he was met by affirmative gestures and felt genuinely supported. He realised that showing vulnerability, as long as there was a commitment to improve something, was not a bad thing, as he had secretly thought before. It actually made him feel stronger and more confident; and he knew it showed.

When Laura judged that Stephen had finished his check-in with his team, she progressed with the exercise.

"Good. Now, we're going to divide into two groups again. We'll have Stephen, JR and Anna in one group, and Sophia, Samuel and Christine in the other. I have a whole bunch of magazines here that I want you to flick through for inspiration. When you see a picture, a word, or something else that you think represents your vision, or is relevant to your purpose, then I want you to cut that out. You will be working both individually and as a group as you do this. When you've exhausted that, I want you to talk about what you've cut out, and why, and start making a collage on your vision boards." Laura pointed towards two big white sheets of paper which had been attached to the wooden panel each side of the window. "When you're done with that, I want you to present your vision board to the other group and to me. Any questions?"

"No, we're good" said Christine and headed over to the table full of magazines, post-it notes, glue, adhesive tape and scissors. "This looks fun!" she exclaimed, pulling her heavy wooden chair up to the table and sitting down.

It didn't take long before they were all flicking through magazines. The sounds of rustling paper, giggles and clipping scissors created a constant wallpaper of sound for the next half hour or so. Eventually they had gone through all the magazines and had several piles of cut-outs in front of them.

"Wow, where do we start?" said JR, turning to Stephen.

Stephen replied: "It's our joint vision we're working on here, so anyone can start. Why don't you start?" He nodded encouragingly to JR.

"OK, I'll try" said JR. He spread out his paper cuttings and rummaged around until he found a picture of a Volvo, driving on a snowy road. He held it up and exclaimed: "We're like this car; we provide a sense of safety for our customers." He picked up another piece of paper where the word FAIR was showing. "We always treat our customers fairly."

"That's quite similar to something I had picked out" continued Anna. She presented a picture of a woman sitting at a table with a cup in her hand and a relieved smile on her face. "We make people feel good" she said simply.

"Good, good" said Stephen and continued by adding some of his thoughts.

At the other table, all eyes were on Samuel, who so far had not been the most forthcoming in any of the exercises they had done.

Samuel looked relaxed as he shared his view by producing a picture of a man in a suit with his arms crossed casually across his chest. "We provide a professional service and we are seen as professional and trustworthy."

Christine showed a photo of a family on holiday, laughing at the camera, with a carefree air. "We make people feel like this", she said simply.

In both groups they continued to show what they had chosen and why. Slowly but surely a number of their clippings made their way onto the wall, creating two unique vision collages. The two groups finished at pretty much the same time and subsequently turned to Laura, asking her to come over to have a look.

Laura walked over to the panelled wall and appraised the results. "Looking good. So tell me about your vision, your purpose", she said to no one in particular.

"Which group would like to go first?"

Stephen decided that this was something he definitely wanted to do, to practice expressing the team's vision, so he stepped forward.

"Our vision, our purpose, is to deliver the best customer service in the insurance industry. Customers will want to be our customers as they know we are always fair, empathetic and take good care of them. They know they are in good hands with us." He pointed to different pictures on the wall, which supported his words, as he spoke.

"Thanks" said Laura. She invited the other group to continue but was met by a stunned silence from Samuel, Sophia and Christine.

Sophia was the first to regain her speaking abilities. "That's uncanny! We have created almost exactly the same vision; similar pictures, the same words, everything. Look at this picture here of the Volvo. We've chosen exactly the same picture! Unbelievable!" She shook her head in amazement.

Stephen, JR and Anna had walked over the other group's collage and were now studying it with great interest. Their reaction was almost identical. "Spooky!" Stephen declared, an incredulous expression on his face.

Laura had already noticed the similarities. It had been very easy for them to come up with this as they had just spent two days focusing and being immersed in how they operated together, not just what they 'did' as a team. There was a phenomenal sense of clarity as they had all been sharing their thoughts throughout this process. Another important part of the Formula.

"You've done a good job. How did you find that exercise?"

Anna was first to respond: "It was surprisingly easy. We realised pretty quickly that we had similar ideas about our purpose and what it is we want to achieve, but putting it down in words and pictures has made it much more tangible and cohesive. It's as if we have a renewed sense of being 'on the same page'. Now that I've seen the other group's collage, I am really impressed that we are so in tune with each other. This must obviously be our vision."

Laura noticed that even Samuel was nodding at this. It was the first time he was proactively agreeing with one of his colleagues.

"Excellent" said Laura. "I think you are ready to pull all your learning's from these 2 days together and move on to your Operating Principles. I want you to discuss how you need to work together to be able to achieve the vision, to fulfil your purpose. How will you function as a team to make it all happen?"

There was silence at first. Everyone was reflective, thinking hard about what this meant and whether they would need to make changes to how they were working to make this happen.

Stephen opened up the discussion: "I think we need to meet regularly and talk properly, not just do status updates."

Anna followed: "Yes, and we should discuss issues and not be afraid to be honest when doing so, as long as we are respectful. We should encourage our teams to do the same, with us, with each other and with others. We need to lead the way on this though, to be role models and show that we mean it."

"Great. And how about helping each other, using our different strengths?" JR contributed.

Further brainstorming took place where the ideas were flowing freely and effortlessly from them. A long list of potential guidelines was drawn up. They finally agreed to commit to the following:

- Answer emails from each other within 24 hours
- Give each other regular, constructive, helpful feedback
- Ask for help when needed
- Share ideas and best practices on a regular basis
- Focus on individual strengths and make the most of them
- Call each other (instead of sending an email, when only 2 persons involved) whenever possible, to minimise endless emails back and forth
- Adhere to communication plan
- Ensure we have team agreement on issues that impact everyone

It came easily to them, it seemed so obvious now.

To support the Operating Guidelines, a Team Communication Plan was created, another part of the Formula. It contained an agreement to meet in person at least twice a year, to have weekly leadership team calls, to implement monthly email updates from Stephen to all employees, along with some minor points.

They were rapidly learning how to be a team, Sophia reflected, and not just a team but a great team. *"Who would have thought?"* she mused.

At the end of the day, a draft document had been drawn up. It outlined what the team was all about, who was responsible for what and how they would work as a team going forward. They all signed the document to visually show their commitment to the agreement. Stephen placed the document resolutely in his briefcase, together with the folded storyboards.

Stephen was beaming, a wide grin from ear to ear. His team had finally arrived in earnest. It was a team he was proud to call himself the leader of, and he knew that they would be able to work together in a much more productive way now. He felt more relaxed than he had felt for a very long time.

"Now you know the Team Formula. You've found your way through the confusing maze of teams. It's time to take that magic back to work" Laura concluded.

*

It was 5.15pm. The team were lingering in the hotel lobby with their suitcases and briefcases. It was still remarkably warm for late September, so there was not a single coat in sight. The only indication of the autumn around the corner was the sun standing lower in the sky than normal for such a warm day.

Sophia jingled her car keys, breaking the spell enough to make it possible for them to leave. They all started picking up their bags and strode towards the door. It was time to go.

Anna was almost sad to leave. So much had happened in the two days. In fact, it felt strange to think that it had only been two days. She hoped with all her being that they would be able to take the magic that had been created here back with them to the office. *"We simply have to"*, she thought. *"We can't have done all of this for nothing, now we need to go do what we've talked about and agreed."*

Once outside the team separated, to cars and waiting taxis, and with the evening sun as their backdrop, they left the old city of learning that had become their own special place of learning.

Stephen's Journal

Wow! I think we've done it! No, correction, I KNOW we've done it, with emphasis on WE because it really has been a team effort. I hadn't previously thought about how much a successful team is lead from within the team, not just by the leader. A leader can only be the guide, the facilitator of that process. A leader can never do it alone if he/she wants a team of people who are fully engaged and intrinsically   motivated.
And we are a now officially a team, and not just that, but a team with a mission, fully aligned and dedicated. Thank you!

I'm strangely tired and adrenaline pumped at the same time. I wonder if I'll be able to sleep. It's 1am already and I'm still buzzing.

I wish Alice had been awake so that I could talk to her about this. She definitely has a part in this success. But it's OK, it can wait until tomorrow. Tomorrow is going to be a good day. I will need to talk to Gerry too and let him know that he was right, the process worked☺.

My only slight question mark is Samuel, still, as usual. Is he really with us? I'm still not 100% sure and I should be by now. I will give him the benefit of the doubt. I'll give him the chance to prove that he's following our agreements from this transforming event. If he doesn't, I will take care of it, resolutely, swiftly. Laura's question about what the team would be like without Samuel has made me acutely aware of his impact on the team and our results. I cannot let him continue to have that impact. He needs to prove himself now and he needs to do it immediately. I think he has moved though, he was definitely different towards the end. I think it got to him.

I am so proud of the other team members too. Christine really opened up and said some things I did not expect. Anna totally demonstrated her support and got some great feedback on how she had a big influence on the team. I was really happy with JR, he realised just how much we all need each other to be successful in our own rights. Sophia threw herself into this task and she is definitely more involved. Everyone is different and contributes in their special way. I feel lucky now that I have such a diverse team, I really appreciate it. I am so pleased. I know I demonstrated my leadership by being vulnerable; it earned a level of respect and built more trust, which is what Laura said it is all about. I have experienced the Team Formula, that's for sure!

Chapter 23: The Payoff

"Culture does not change because we desire to change it. Culture changes when the organization is transformed; the culture reflects the realities of people working together every day".

Frances Hesselbein

It was the month of May, a very busy time for Stephen. He had come into the office early to catch up on his emails from the day before, some of which he had not yet had time to read. He was just about to open his inbox when the phone rang. Helmut's name appeared on the screen. It was unusual for Helmut to call unless something really important had happened, and rarely this early, so Stephen snatched up his phone, answering it quickly.

"Good morning, Helmut"

"Good morning to you, Stephen" responded Helmut with a hint of a smile in his voice.

Stephen was intrigued now.

"It's just a quick call to say well done and congratulations. You have been nominated for a Chairman's Award, in the Teamwork category."

"Really? Where did that come from?"

"The Global Head of Sales nominated you and your team for working together so effectively that one of our customers claims he has become an ambassador for our company. He gives you and your team the credit for that. It seems you all pulled together and helped this customer in a way that he had never experienced before. Excellent work! His company has now given us their entire insurance portfolio. I don't know how you've done it but whatever you've done, it has certainly worked. You have turned that team around and you've become a leader. Well done. I'll keep my fingers crossed that you get the award."

Helmut was not a man of many words, always brief and to the point, and this call was no exception. After telling Stephen that the nomination wording was making its way to him in an email, they ended their conversation. Stephen leapt up and punched the air with his fist, shouting: "YES, YES, YES!" He felt like his face would crack from the big smile on it. He wanted to tell someone, he wanted to share this.

"Who should I call? Who's in? Or wait a minute, maybe I need to read the nomination first?" He chuckled.

He turned around and leaned over to reach his laptop, pressing the 'send/receive' button to refresh his inbox. The screen flickered to refresh and then the email was there. Stephen clicked on the email and then the attachment, which wouldn't download straight away. He jumped up and down in anticipation. *"Come on!"* he thought. Finally it appeared.

Nomination for Chairman's Award

Category: Teamwork

Describe the nominee's extraordinary contribution and why you think they should receive this award:

The Global Customer Service Team, lead by Stephen, has shown exceptional teamwork by working tirelessly across different locations to deliver a whole new level of service. They use a coordinated approach, each sharing the information they have with each other, which means they have a good overview at any time. This in turn means that they can change direction swiftly to meet and exceed customer expectations in a fast-changing marketplace. They take responsibility at an individual and a team level instead of apportioning blame. An example of this is reflected in feedback from a customer with a complex global set-up, where we as a company had previously not been able to coordinate such complexity. This team managed to pull it together to the degree that the customer wrote an article about their experience in a business journal entitled "How I became an ambassador for my insurance company".

Stephen continued to read through the nomination and when he came to the end, he felt a sense of pride and recognition that he had simply not felt before.

Stephen's Journal

I don't really mind if we don't win the Chairman's Award. It's just great to have been nominated (I know they always say that at the Oscar's ceremony, but I really mean it!☺). It's the biggest recognition I could ever get for what the team and I have achieved.

I feel like I've created a legacy that will last beyond my leadership. The team is now team run; we have a shared responsibility that just wasn't there before.

When I think back to last summer, when I started to plan this with Laura, I learned I had to believe in the team development journey to make the others believe in it, even though I wasn't sure how it was going to go. I had to act 'as if' I fully believed in it, which is very powerful. When you act 'as if', you create the mindset that will actually make it all a reality. It is so worth it!

Chapter 24: Different perspectives

"Tell me and I forget, teach and I may remember, involve and I learn"

Benjamin Franklin

JR was in the middle of his quick morning coffee ritual on his way to work. The café was on the ground floor of his office building. The smell of coffee always stimulated his thinking in new directions. He had been lucky to get a small table by the window, through which he could observe the myriad of people, all in a hurry to get somewhere.

"A year ago, when we first met as a team in the Archipelago things were very different. I was so used to working independently, thinking that's how I would be successful. I had never considered just how much I could learn from my colleagues and how they could help me. I have grown more this year than in any twelve month period before. A big part of that is how much more open to others' opinions I am now, which is entirely thanks to us coming together as a team and sharing views, feedback and experience. I have realised that no one can go it alone. I listen better and in the process, I have become much more knowledgeable and have more options in any given situation. Although I think I was always quite good at getting people with me, this is so much more marked now. I seem to be able to get people really engaged and motivated. I think listening plays a major part in this result. I'm pleased I told Stephen, in our one-to-one last week, what an impact the work we've done as a team has had on me as a leader. I have particularly enjoyed how we are now

using everyone's strengths recognising that everyone contributes in their unique way. I am now part of a confident, driven and successful team. I like that."

JR's phone vibrated on the table, indicating the arrival of a text message. His focus was brought back to the day's events as he read his message. *"I wonder what today will bring."*

*

Samuel stepped off his train and took a deep breath of fresh air. It felt good to have left the city behind. He had had a busy day and he was beginning his winding down time. It was the end of the rush hour so he could easily make his way along the platform, down the stairs and towards the car park, without having to weave in and out of his fellow commuters.

It was close to the longest day of the year, it had been sunny all day and the smell of hot leather filled his nostrils as he opened the car door. On his drive home his mind travelled back through the previous year.

"I have to give Stephen some credit. We are a better team today than we were a year ago. There's still more we can do, but it is better. Most importantly we are delivering better results. We trust each other so we share more information and can make decisions faster. I must admit that this has worked so well that I have taken it back to my direct reports and I am encouraging a greater exchange there too. It works. I think I've learned another thing here. It wasn't very smart of me to go behind Stephen's back to Helmut. The effect of that

was quite dramatic, much more than I had imagined, and I frankly didn't get as much out of it as I had hoped. I'm not going to do that again, it backfired on me and I don't want to experience that again. Maybe there are limits to how straight people can be though? Do I really want to work like this? I know it's working in a way, but is it for me?"

Samuel turned into his drive and parked his car squarely in front of his garage. He sat still for a moment, his eyes fixed on the garage door as he took stock of his situation.

*

One day a week Christine was working from home. This was one of those days. She was always pleasantly surprised at how much she got done when distractions were minimised. At the same time she missed the social interaction of the office, especially the way it had been working lately. Her big desk was a mixture of order and chaos, with a long to do-list and piles and piles of paper. Her window was shaded by a tall, thin fir tree with the ends of the branches pointing downwards. The tree moved gently in the wind, making the shadow dance back and forth, catching her eye. Christine finished her call with Anna and rocked back in her plush chair.

"It's so much easier for me to do my job well now. I can just pick up the phone and talk directly to any of my colleagues to sort out any problems immediately. Because I know them better, I am more comfortable picking up the phone. Because they know me better, they are more willing to listen to my suggestions. I also make better

suggestions now that I don't fear their reaction to what I say. It's a never-ending cycle, where one person's behaviour positively impacts the other person's behaviour. The Team Formula works! We all used to be defensive in our own corners. Now there are no corners as we are all on the same side. The openness between me and my colleagues has made me feel stronger and better equipped to deal with this divorce that I've been through. I can't believe I ended up eventually talking to them about it. I must really trust them! They've been a great support to me in that respect, even though they may not realise it. Maybe I need to tell them?"

*

Anna was preparing for a meeting with the local sales team in Stockholm. Her office overlooked Nybroviken where the tour boats were filling up with tourists eager to see the city from the water, often the best angle. Anna took a break from her preparations and gazed dreamily at the boat that had just slipped its moorings, heading out of the bay. She loved the summer and never tired of this view. The meeting ahead provided yet another opportunity for Anna to influence the sales team, to create the best possible experience for their customers. She used to keep a low profile in these meetings, thinking that her opinions weren't valued or valuable, but the last year had changed all of that. Anna had changed significantly and had rightfully claimed her place at the table. People had noticed it and had given her recognition for it. The words of the Sales Director had stuck in her mind: "Thank you, Anna, for playing an active role in our meetings. Your comments have been an eye-opener for us and I don't think we would have been able to sign the corporate deal last month without the benefit of your experience."

"I never realised how much others could learn from me. I didn't think it could make that big a difference, or that I had that much to contribute. Being encouraged to share my observations, thoughts and feelings in the safe team environment in Oxford last autumn gave me new confidence to express myself. I've not only used it in that team and with my direct reports, but I've now applied it to all areas of my life. Another learning from Oxford was the importance of having healthy conflict, expressing differences of opinion. The tensions are gone as we now address issues in an open way. It feels better to come to work. The sales director has actually asked for my advice on how to create a similar team success for his team! How cool is that! Yes, I'm more than happy to share the Formula with them. I can't wait to be a part of that as it will further strengthen the co-operation between our two teams."

She smiled as she left for her meeting.

*

Sophia returned from lunch and woke up her computer. Unlike most people, she considered the hour after lunch one of the most productive in the day, so whenever possible she blocked it for reflection time. There was a crunching sound as she bit into the crispy, green apple that was her dessert. The open office space around her was only half full due to the time of the day. She smiled when she saw one of her business partners manoeuvring the door in an awkward way, balancing too many coffees on a tray. Disaster was avoided as another person rushed to hold the door. A familiar scene.

"I learned so much from the Team Formula, with Stephen and his leadership team. I knew straight away that I wanted to use the same Formula with the team I lead as well. With the geographical challenges, the Formula has brought us much closer together, just as it did for the leadership team at River Castle. The new, clear alignment has made my leadership role easier, or it's freed up time for me to be more of a supportive leader, rather than someone who needs to get involved in everything. I learned from Stephen how you can be a leader and a team member at the same time. It has also really paid off to have a regular slot in our team calls to keep it alive. I get the feeling that the perception of the team has improved internally too. Oh, that reminds me, I need to contact JR and check how my buddy is doing."

She tapped his name to message him.

*

Stephen slowly put his mobile phone down, staring at the disappearing number on the screen. *A headhunter!* His head was spinning. The call had created an internal turmoil of massive proportions. Not once had he anticipated getting a call like that. He had been so busy with the renewed confidence given to him and his team that he hadn't considered the perception their success had created outside the company. The head-hunter had said that he had been identified as someone with strong leadership capabilities in bringing a team together, working together and creating customer ambassadors.

He sprung out of his chair and walked purposefully over to the window. He raised his hands to the back of his head and locked his fingers together, looking up at the ceiling.

"What a job! What an opportunity! I can hardly believe it! It seems almost too good to be true. To be offered a job that wants me to both create a new global customer strategy **and** *deliver it.*

But I don't want to leave my team, we are such a great team, we've come a long way together. I've taken this team on a developing journey, the extent of which I didn't quite comprehend from the beginning. I just didn't know what I didn't know before we started all this. I've given them a set of transportable, transferable team skills, which they can take anywhere. If I leave, I know they are more than capable of carrying on without me. On the other hand, there is more we could do together. We have some interesting challenges ahead. I can't leave them.

Yet the job is perfect for me. I think I would love it and I would be good at it. It would definitely be a major promotion, a senior position. What a dilemma! What should I do?"

THE END

Now, let's make use of this book...

The Team Formula:

Get together as a team

+

Get to know each other much deeper, creating trust

+

Really talk to each other, openly, be courageous

+

Give each other behavioural TOP feedback

+

Build on individual and team strengths, creating drive and self-esteem

+

Agree on your team purpose and direction

+

Decide how to work together and how to measure success

+

Be generous, fearlessly share what you know with your colleagues

+

Commit to what's been agreed together

+

Keep your promise, hold each other accountable

=

Team Success

Summary and Key Learning Points

Everyone will take their own learning from what they read, hear, watch or experience. Whatever learning or ideas YOU take from this book, they will be what you need and what's relevant for you right now.

In this section we have summarised some of the key learning points from our point of view, which you might also find useful. It acts as a brief summary of the book.

ON TEAM LEADERSHIP

- There are two ways to lead a team. First, letting people get on with their jobs individually with very little "team" interaction or guidance from you. Second, being a proactive leader, providing the team with the direction and structure and culture that can allow it to be a great team. This book is about the second way, the proactive way.

- Getting a team to work well together requires work up front. Leaders rarely feel they have the time for this, particularly if they are going through a time-consuming change process, but it is definitely an investment that pays off, and quicker than you would think. If you can get your team fully aligned, working well together, you will be able to deliver better results quicker.

ON CHANGE

- During takeovers and mergers people feel allegiance with their old brand, which creates two camps, often pulling in different directions. It's extra important in those scenarios to quickly get the team together to explore their new joint purpose and direction. Otherwise the divide will be allowed to grow bigger and it can take longer to get the team off to a new start.

- In times of change people tend to focus on the stories and the "grapevine" which can distract getting the job done. Human nature means people start to talk about what might happen rather than the reality. Leaders need to work hard at keeping people informed and communicating whatever they can. They also need to engage people, give them whatever direction they can and a future focus. This keeps people motivated and productive through uncertain times. Communicate more not less. People want to feel valued and to understand what is happening while having as much communication as possible. Getting people together and discussing what is happening and how people feel is critical to ride the wave of change. Otherwise people feel they are in a maze and don't know which way to go.

ON COMMUNICATION AND MEETINGS

- When preparing for a meeting, don't just focus on what you are going to say and do, also consider how you will do it. Think about the other people who will be in the meeting, the dynamic between people and how you can prepare to best manage that dynamic.

- In meetings, be aware of the dynamics between people and the unsaid messages. Listen, observe and feel what is going on to improve your chances to be able to manage the meeting most effectively.

- Communication is about more than the words. Much of communication is non-verbal, in the form of body language and facial expressions. The tone of voice used will also send a message, often stronger than the actual words. Consider the difference of "What do you mean?" said in a friendly voice and a smile or said with a loud voice, stern facial look while leaning forward. Practice using your observation skills to "read" the situation or "read between the lines", rather than just listening to the words. Become an expert at really hearing what people are saying. Don't be too quick to jump to conclusions though – always ask for clarification when possible.

- A team effectiveness event, such as the one Stephen had with his team in Oxford, is different to traditional team building, as the aim is to create a real change in team behaviours rather than just become more comfortable with each other, as a team.

- If you plan to run a team effectiveness event, keep in mind that it's best if you can take the team offsite for the session. When people leave their office behind, it creates a more focused, closer climate and results can be achieved quicker. Getting away from the office can help people to break free from old thinking patterns and provide greater solutions.

ON TEAM TIME

- The environment for meetings and team events matter. The right environment and atmosphere can impact the results of a meeting. For example, if you hold a meeting in a room with no daylight and at the same time you want people to be energized and creative, you're unlikely to get the results you want.

- The time a team spends together is valuable, too valuable to just leave to chance. On top of that, everyone's individual time is important, so you want to make sure you respect that. Think about what the team's mission is, and what the team members would be best doing when together to maximize teamwork and results. If there are things that don't add value to the team meetings or calls, don't do them there. Some updates may be more efficient to simply send in an email for everyone to read in their own time, rather than taking up productive team time. When team time is focused on the right things, the team members will feel that they leave the meeting richer than before, richer in awareness, knowledge, experience and performance.

- Share best practices within the team, and other teams if relevant. There's no reason to reinvent the wheel. It's a great way to reduce rework and duplication, and it can greatly improve productivity.

ON FEEDBACK AND BEHAVIOURS

- When performing a Team Climate Survey, like Laura did when she interviewed the team members ahead of the Oxford team session, it's of vital importance to clearly communicate how the process will work. It's of particular importance to stress that the process is completely confidential, so no individual comments can be traced back to the individual. This helps people to give honest feedback on the team climate. If you don't get the honest feedback, then what's the point?

- When it comes to the work a team does, its leader needs to focus on behaviours, in addition to tasks. Work is not just about "what we do", the tasks – it's also, and potentially more importantly, about "how we do it", the behaviours.   Many organisations attempt to focus on behaviours through the use of identified competencies, which may or may not form a part of the performance appraisal process.   But that is not enough. Behaviours need to be observed regularly and people need to be made aware of the effect their behaviours will have on the tasks. And the effects are equally seen in the relationships with customers, colleagues, partners, senior managers, the community and all other stakeholders, and ultimately the results they get.

- It's difficult, even close to impossible, to truly view yourself from the outside, to see the impact of your behaviours. Ask for feedback from the relevant people around you, preferably those that see you often enough to be able to give you a fair picture. And accept the feedback gracefully, even if you get to hear something you didn't want to hear. Otherwise people will not be so forthcoming with feedback next time around. Feedback allows for a person to "step out" and take a more objective look at themselves. Consider the benefits of knowing your own impact on the people and world around you. Without it, you just don't know how you're doing and may be continuing to do things that just don't work. And maybe more importantly, you don't know when you are doing something really well and should keep doing it! It's easy for us all to have "blind spots".

- Consider what you can do to foster a climate of feedback within the team too. Make people aware of the benefits of feedback. Encourage open, trusting discussions. Make sure that feedback focuses both on things that work well and on things that could be improved. Use the TOP Feedback formula (from chapter 21).

- Think about how you and your team view your main stakeholders, keeping in mind that the team members are indeed each other's stakeholders too. How we look at others will impact how we behave towards them. If you want your team to treat others well, they need to view them in a positive, accepting, constructive way. And it needs to start 'at home', within the team, they need to view and treat each other as important people. Treat each other as customers!

ON JOURNALING

- The use of a journal, somewhere to capture thoughts, ideas, experiences and insights is an effective way of developing your thinking, solving problems and learning new things. Writing something down takes 100% concentration and in doing so, you both focus your mind and get a new perspective by seeing your thoughts in writing. Journaling could take place daily or weekly to be most effective. Find a time of day where it suits you best to write and get stuck in! Make it simple, make it easy, it doesn't need to be fancy or follow any set structure. It doesn't have to take more than a few minutes, and the rewards can be great.

ON CONFLICTS AND PROBLEMS

- Conflict and tension is a must in teams, it's needed to progress a team through to effectiveness. To harness the power of conflict and tension, you need to find ways of resolving them, rather than just sweeping them under the carpet. What conflict is after all, is a difference in view, opinion. By viewing conflict that way, and insisting on respectful behaviours between people, you can de-dramatize these differences and focus the team members' attention towards solutions.

- If an agreement has been made within a team, it is paramount that you hold team members to account to those agreements. If you don't do this, you will create a sense of distrust in the team and undermine your own leadership. When you hold people accountable, you are showing them that you are "walking the talk", you are not full of buzz words, and you actually value and recognise when people do the right thing. This will in turn encourage people to do the right thing next time, and you start to create a culture of follow-through and performance. Agreements can of course, just as importantly, also be about behaviours; acceptable and non-acceptable behaviours.

- Part of the success that the team in the book achieved was down to connecting with each other on an emotional level. They didn't just *understand* how to work as a team, they experienced it on an emotional level. This was created through a high level of personal disclosure, daring to be vulnerable and being open to understanding their own impact on the others.

- If there is a problem, address it in a respectful and timely way. No real problem will become easier to solve with time, it's better to deal with it as soon as possible. The exception might be smaller problems, which may just resolve themselves over time and do not need attention.

ON TRUST

- To create trust in a team, you obviously need to keep promises to each other, being trustworthy. But it's also about giving something of yourself. You need to be vulnerable and show courage. To demonstrate courage is to show more of who you really are, not just your work persona or your polished image. You need to show trust to get trust.

- Not all company cultures are open and trusting. If openness and trust is lacking where you work, then it starts with you. You need to decide what you're comfortable sharing, to encourage greater exchange and trust. Sharing work knowledge and experience can be a good and safe place to start.

ON LEADERSHIP

- No one has all the answers. Be open to others' ideas and experience, there's always a lot to learn from others, not just people senior to you. Most leaders feel they have to have all the answers. This is an impossible expectation! Relax and allow everyone to contribute, because if you don't have the answer, someone else will or you will find it together.

- Show flexibility in leadership. Use your observation skills to decide what approach is most effective with the person you are communicating with, keeping in mind that everyone is different. You've heard the expression "different strokes for different folks" – it's very true. In the case of Stephen and Samuel when Stephen needed to confront Samuel about going behind his back (chapter 10), Stephen had realised that he needed to be firm, direct and to the point with Samuel. A softer approach is unlikely to have worked as well in this situation.

- If you want a committed team, everyone needs to be responsible for the solutions and the results of the team. A leader can't do it alone, nor should he/she. People are motivated through involvement and ownership, to feel they have a say, that they are important and can make a difference. An effective team is not just lead by a leader, it is lead by the whole team, guided and supported by the leader.

- Just like people, teams are unique. Every team is different. Each team's challenges and contributions are surprisingly unique. As a result, the route is different for each team but the team formula is there to help you and the team figure out your unique roadmap. You find that you can't get through the maze on your own. You need the collective intelligence, experience, ideas and drive of the whole team to get there. That's when things happen.

- One final thought. As a leader you need to believe that this will work (not just intellectually, but actually feel it in your gut), because what you believe with conviction drives your actions and results. If you believe with conviction, so will the team, and then you will get there. Are *you* ready to make a move? Let's go.

Discussion Questions

Now you have read this book, please go ahead and make the most of it by reflecting on some of these questions and applying learning to yourself and to your team.

If you lead a team or if you are a part of a team, then it is a great exercise to ask your team to read the book in preparation for a meeting. You can then hold a meeting with the team and discuss these questions and agree on actions.

You may want to use all of the questions or choose a few that you and the team can relate to.

LEADER QUESTIONS FOR LEADERS

1. What could Stephen have done differently to demonstrate more effective leadership?
2. What did he do that *did* demonstrate effective leadership?
3. What learning could you take from Stephen's approach that can apply to you?
4. How does writing a journal help Stephen? What does he gain from it? How could it help you?
5. How do you talk to your team or colleagues? Are you a straight talker, like the straight talking in the article?
6. How could you take more responsibility for your relationship with your boss? Where is it on scale of 1 - 10 and where does it need to be?

7. How much valuable feedback are you giving to others and receiving from others? How can you improve this?

8. How clearly are you communicating to the people around you? In what way and how could that be more impactful?

9. How do you communicate change? How are you considering the impact of the change on others?

10. What is the perception of you as a leader? What do you want it to be? What is your own personal vision of you as a leader?

11. What are you doing to develop and increase trust levels in your team?

12. Who is your trusted advisor? Do you have someone you can talk to and confide in, who is outside of your everyday environment? How could you make that happen? What would you gain from that?

13. When did you last demonstrate your vulnerability? How and in what way? Could you do more of that?

14. Are you being authentic in your leadership? Is the best of you coming out for others to experience?

15. How does Alice support and help Stephen? Where can you find support in your personal life?

16. What else did you learn from this book for yourself? How can you apply The Team Formula?

TEAM QUESTIONS FOR THE TEAM

17. What did you learn from this book? What "aha-moments" did you have?

18. How could you be more proactive as a team at working on "HOW" you operate as a team?

19. Does Stephen's team need to be a team? Why? What is the compelling reason?

20. Does your team need to be a team? Why? What is the compelling reason?

21. How does environment affect and impact a team? What is the environment like when you meet? Where do you meet and when?

22. What are the climate and the atmosphere like in your team when you are together?

23. What do you see as the strengths of your team? And the developments for the team?

24. What is the time like that you spend together? Is it valuable and useful? How could it be enhanced?

25. What useful behaviours are being demonstrated within your team? How can you maximize them? What un-useful behaviours are being demonstrated? How do you want to change those behaviours?

26. How well do you know each other? What could you do to get to know each other better?

27. What is the current perception of your team? If you were to go and ask people around you, what would they say? What do you want them to say going forward?

28. How does your team members communicate with each other? How well do you seem to support each other? How well aligned are you?

29. How well do people support each other across departments and functions? How does the team role model this? (How much encouragement is there of cross-functional work or are there silo behaviours?)

30. How does the team make decisions? What is the impact on you and others?

31. How clear are roles and responsibilities? What needs to happen and what are the impacts?

32. How does the team deal with Samuel and the conflict when he betrays the team? What could they have done differently and what could Stephen have done differently?

33. What happens when you all make an agreement in your team? Does everyone stick to it? How could you enhance that? What agreements do you need to make?

34. How are you holding each other accountable? How could you start to do that more?

35. If you have any team agreements, are they at a behavioural level? How could you make them more behavioural?

36. Does your team have a clear vision and direction? How could you create one?

37. How do problems and issues get handled in your team?

38. What are trust levels like in your team? How can you increase them?

39. What else can you as a team learn from this book and apply? How can you apply The Team Formula?

40. How could you use the TOP Feedback formula as a team?

Enjoy discussing these as a team and give yourself enough time to explore the responses and have some good, open dialogue. Continue to review the questions and keep coming back to them over time. Use these along with The Team Formula to create a great team.

Have fun and enjoy the journey.

About the Authors

Mandy Flint

Mandy is an International Expert on leading and developing teams. Mandy is the CEO of Excellence in Leadership, a global transformational change organisation which she founded in 2000 after over 20 years of leadership experience in the corporate world. During this time Mandy spent 14 years working for American Express running business units and held roles in sales operations, public affairs, communications and cultural change.

As well as leading a business division within American Express as a senior leader Mandy spent 3 years leading a cultural change transformation programme for the President as well as operating as an internal coach and team coach to many senior executive teams.

Through Excellence in Leadership Mandy works across the globe with both teams and individuals in the areas of one-to-one executive coaching, group training, team effectiveness, vision creation, strategic development and cultural change management. Her clients include CEOs, SVP's, VPs and Board members in many multi-national blue-chip organisations, including MasterCard, Lloyds, American Express, Symantec, Virgin Atlantic, Hewlett Packard, SAP, G4, the NHS and Reuters.

Mandy has studied at Harvard Business School focusing on the concept of the Service Profit Chain and has certification in the Tavistock Programme specialising in Advanced Process Consultancy. She is also media-trained and is an established speaker at leadership and cultural change events.

Mandy lives in Sussex, UK with her family.

Elisabet Vinberg Hearn

Elisabet has extensive experience from the business world, including 13 years with American Express, based both in Sweden and in the UK. She has held various leadership roles, responsible for customer servicing, process re-engineering and corporate culture transformation.

She's CEO of Think Solutions UK Ltd in the UK and Think Solutions AB in Sweden, leadership consultancies specialising in employee engagement and profitable corporate cultures. She also actively operates as a consultant, speaker and coach, providing strategic leadership and tactical solutions to clients around the World. Her consulting experience includes Executive Coaching, Leadership, Team Dynamics and Effectiveness, Transformational Communication, Customer Service, Cultural Change, Cultural Intelligence, Visioning and Strategic Development. She has worked with individuals, leaders and teams in numerous companies around the world, including ABN AMRO, Royal Bank of Scotland, American Express, H&M, IKEA, Skanska, Vattenfall, Trygg-Hansa (Royal Sun Alliance) and Bombardier Transportation and others.

She has a degree in Marketing Economics from IHM Business School and is currently (Jan 2013) working on her dissertation for an MBA in Leadership and Sustainability at the Robert Kennedy College/University of Cumbria.

Elisabet lives with her family in Stockholm, Sweden.